The Occ

The Occult and You

ROGER ELLIS

Authentic
LIFESTYLE

08 07 06 05 04   7 6 5 4 3 2 1

First published 1989 by Kingsway Publications Ltd.
This edition published 2004 by Authentic Media,
9 Holdom Avenue, Bletchley, Milton Keynes, Bucks MK1 1QR, UK
and PO Box 1047, Waynesboro, GA 30830–2047, USA.

British Library Cataloguing in Publication Data
A catalogue record for this book is available from the British Library

ISBN 1-86024-473-4

Cover Design by David Lund
Typeset by Waverley Typesetters, Galashiels
Print Management by Adare Carwin
Printed and Bound in Denmark by Nørhaven Paperback

Dedication

To all those whose calling and commitment is to work with young people. People like Dan, Kate and Ellie. All youth workers, church planters, counsellors and befrienders. I salute you! You're the best!

Contents

Foreword

At boarding school I was trying to get to sleep but at the other end of the dormitory three of the boys were whispering excitedly. I knew that they had borrowed the Scrabble letters from the common room earlier that day and were now trying to contact spirits through a home-made Ouija board. I didn't know what to do – no one at church had ever taught me what the Bible says about the occult – so I just tried to get to sleep.

Suddenly there was a commotion – a stifled scream and pandemonium. One of the boys later claimed he'd seen a terrifying green light emerge from the Ouija board and zoom down the long dormitory. I don't know if that really happened or if he was imagining it, but I do know that the whole room was suddenly charged with fear: real and dark.

The housemaster simply laughed the episode off as teenage delusion. The school chaplain seemed to think it was wonderful that boys were engaging at all with spiritual things – and then offered me a cigarette!

It would be a few more years before I would get my head around such things from a Christian point of view, learning about the reality of the occult on one hand and the greater reality of God's supernatural power on the other. One of the key people to explain such things to me from the Bible was Roger Ellis. I was fascinated by Roger's personal experiences of spiritual warfare, deliverance and Revelation Church's effective witness to many caught up in the dangerous web of occult fascination. But there was nothing spooky about Roger: he was earthy, funny, practical, prayerful and brimming with reassuring swathes of common sense.

More recently, the supernatural goings on at another English boarding school has captured the public imagination to an extraordinary extent. Harry Potter has introduced us to a mystical world full of 'good' magic and the dark powers of Lord Vordemort. In some other existence, Tolkien's white wizard Gandalf reminds us that 'The eye of the enemy is moving', in an epic struggle against Sauron for Middle Earth. Programmes like *Buffy the Vampire Slayer* have turned paganism into one of the fastest growing playground religions with books of magic spells marketed specifically at teenagers. And far from the realms of science fiction fantasy, we have the persistent power of astrology in a new generation of celebrity glossies – and in the newspapers, chilling accounts of ritually abused bodies such as the one found in 2003 in the River Thames.

It seems that our fascination with the dark side is back with a vengeance. Not so many years ago some Christians doubted the very existence of a supernatural realm. I remember reading a Bible commentary from the 1930s in which a well-respected scholar was expounding Matthew 8:28–34 – the story of the man whose demons are cast into a neighbouring herd of pigs. Embarrassed by the idea of a demonic realm, the writer argued that Jesus had commanded the demons to leave the man with such a very loud shout that the pigs were terrified and so they all, simultaneously, committed suicide by jumping off a cliff. I don't know much about pig farming, but such porky paranoia sounds a bit unlikely to me! It seems much easier just to take the Bible at face value and accept that the world really is a battlefield between demons and angels, good and evil, God and the devil, prayer and the occult.

But as the world wakes up spiritually to the powers of darkness, few Christians know how to respond. Some seem to be in denial about the power of the occult, convinced that the devil will play by our middle class, middle-of-the-road and middle-aged rules so as to avoid upsetting anyone. Others are going stark, raving bonkers and spotting demons in everything from hair braids to bar codes. Christians at a recent rock festival even prayed against the light-hearted glam rock band The Darkness – having assumed from the name that they must be something sinister to do with the occult without ever having listened to their music!

So Roger Ellis' book is a brilliant, timely guide that will navigate many through the minefield of the contemporary spiritual battlefield. In fact it does more than help us survive. It helps us to laugh, to take ourselves a little less seriously and take the power of the cross a lot more seriously. This book turns a potential minefield into an exciting mission field, ripe for harvest.

Roger is a friend, a mentor, and a man I have watched close up over many years in private and not just on platforms. I can tell you now that he wears manky slippers around the house, thinks Jim Carrey is hilarious, is a great dad almost all of the time and loves God with all his heart. Sometimes when Roger reads the Bible I have heard his voice crack and seen his eyes well with tears. This is a man who practises what he preaches. In fact he practises more than he preaches. Read this book with an open heart because it comes from a man who knows what he's talking about and has proven himself worthy of the gospel over many years.

Roger writes with clarity, simplicity and humour, belying his deep understanding of the theological currents below. The early church father Origen (AD 185–232) pointed out that – when it comes to dealing with the occult – Christians simply call on the name of Jesus and quote Scripture 'while magicians use other names and incantations'. Almost two thousand years later our approach to the occult is still the same. We call on the name of Jesus and we anchor ourselves in Scripture. I think Origen would approve of the book in your hands: it is biblical both in content and in its conviction that victory can be ours when we call on the name of Jesus:

> That at the name of Jesus every knee should bow,
> in heaven and on earth and under the earth,
> and every tongue confess that Jesus Christ is Lord,
> to the glory of God the Father.
>
> (Phil. 2:10, 11)

Chapter 1

A Satellite Picture

Another typical summer's day! Weather ranging from boiling hot sun and clear skies, to black thunderstorms driven by gale-force southerly gusts. Equipment for a day's outing needs to range from shades, sandals and shorts, to wellies, Walkmans and waterproofs!

The lot of the British day-tripper is not a happy one. Never mind – we have the technology, the expertise, and the person from the Met Office to predict for us exactly what's in store for the near future! We all huddle round the 'one-eyed god' (TV set to the uninitiated) and share the delights of the computerised satellite picture.

Firstly apologies for the fact that the only similarity between yesterday's forecast and today's review is the map of Britain. Apparently the 'revelation' we have all been waiting for is that the high pressure band from the Atlantic is just about to get its isobars in a twist with the low pressure band from the North Sea, causing chaos in Cobham, bedlam in Bognor and euphoria in Exeter (which has experienced record temperatures for that time of year). Also, the international picture is a bit shaky: a tropical storm is gathering in the Pacific meaning the outlook is 'unpredictable'. We are 'in the lap of the gods'.

I lean back in my chair, feeling I'd have been better off without the forecast, and grasp the TV remote control hoping to find something more interesting.

A chat show. Okay, I'll give it a try. Subject: the occult. One of the 'new breed' of astrologers (who writes in magazines and appears on breakfast TV) explains: 'It's a new moon, and Saturn moving into line with Pluto will unsettle things, meaning that Sagittarians need to consider that change of relationship, job or location that's been on their minds.' It all sounded a bit like the weather forecast to me.

Next on was a well-known spiritualist medium: an affable, plausible type, seemingly. He is supposedly a Christian but talks little of Jesus Christ and much about messages from spirit guides for people in the audience. *The Simpsons* are on the other side (of the TV that is). That sounds more entertaining – I think I'll turn over!

What's this bloke on about, you ask? First the weather, then the occult. Well, let me explain.

What I am not trying to do is identify the science of meteorology (weather forecasting) with the occult, but merely to draw some comparisons between the two (apologies to all weatherpersons). We will see in this book that the occult is as varied as the weather, both in this country and across the world. Yet the occult scene is strangely linked globally. In certain circumstances it is the same low-pressure area that soaks both America and the UK. The difference between the two cloudbursts will be the amount of refuelling done by the clouds over the Atlantic. Many beliefs in spiritualism, yoga, witchcraft, horoscopes, Ouija boards and the like can be found in countries as far apart as Russia, America and India. As we will see, they are potentially dangerous as they seduce humanity into trying to manipulate 'elements' and 'forces' that are out of its control.

Why the Big Deal?

Day by day our senses are bombarded by propaganda out of the occult stable: books on spiritualism, newspaper reports on the paranormal, horoscopes on the radio and entire magazines dedicated to the supernatural. Many a TV thriller or Hollywood blockbuster carries an occult theme. Police consult mediums when searching for missing bodies, and the Royal Family have some links with Freemasonry.

To the detached observer it may seem strange that people are being drawn to the occult in such vast numbers. What is the attraction? What is the appeal? Well I believe it capitalises on some of our basic needs as human beings. Let us explore these.

The need to worship

Wherever you travel, be it East or West, the so-called Third World or to the heart of Europe, humanity's fascination with worship is plainly obvious. There are shrines dedicated to idols, temples of every religion, as well as many beautiful cathedrals and places set aside for Christian worship. To the atheist it is a sign of humanity in our ignorance and weakness creating a crutch on which we can depend in the face of death. The French philosopher, Voltaire, declared boldly that the progress of science and humanity's intellectual 'evolution' would soon prove a belief in God totally ridiculous. The irony is that many years after Voltaire's death one of his former residences in France is now used by the Bible Society as the location of a printing press for Bibles! The development of the god of science has not made Christianity or the occult obsolete. On the contrary, an awareness of a spiritual realm outside of our physical limitations is certainly on the increase.

To the Christian, of course, this is no surprise. Right from the beginning of the Bible, in the book of Genesis, it is clear that humanity was created by God, to rule and steward the earth and enjoy the privilege of relationship with him. Our preoccupation with worship is a reflection of our deep need of relationship with God, the ultimate purpose for which we were created. Humanity without God is like a car without oil – going nowhere. However, things get even worse when we turn away from God through ignorance, weakness or deliberate rebellion and towards spiritual fulfilment in the occult.

The wrath of God is being revealed from heaven against all the godlessness and wickedness of men who suppress the truth by their wickedness, since what may be known about God is plain to them, because God has made it plain to them. For since the creation of the world God's invisible qualities – his eternal power and divine nature – have been clearly seen, being understood from what has been made, so that men are without excuse.

For although they knew God, they neither glorified him as God nor gave thanks to him, but their thinking became futile and their foolish hearts were darkened. Although they claimed to be wise, they became fools and exchanged the glory of the immortal God for images made to look like mortal man and birds and animals and reptiles.

Therefore God gave them over in the sinful desires of their hearts to sexual impurity for the degrading of their bodies with one another. They exchanged the truth of God for a lie, and worshipped and served created things rather than the Creator – who is forever praised. Amen. (Rom. 1:18–25).

In this passage, the apostle Paul explains that God has revealed himself to humanity through creation. However, the cost of making God number one, and the call to humble ourselves before him, has often proved too much. It is at this stage that people have turned from true worship of the living God towards occult practices and idol worship. Such practices will invoke God's displeasure and often produce a 'bitter harvest' in peoples' lives.

The desire for power

One of the temptations Satan laid before Eve was the possession of power. It was not the power of managing the earth, already given to humanity (Gen. 1:26); but the option of the first revolution, the opportunity of being like God, becoming as powerful as God, 'For God knows that when you eat of it . . . you will be like God, knowing good and evil' (Gen. 3:5). Much of the occult today offers humanity 'enlightenment', 'realisation' or 'godhood'. It is attractive to think that by meditation, understanding our horoscopes, having our tea leaves read, or a seemingly harmless turn of tarot cards, we can have insight into our future, we can be saved from oncoming difficulty, and ensure ourselves success, be it in business, life or relationships. There's something reassuring about being in control, not at the mercy of circumstance or time. And even when the ugly, sobering face of death intervenes there are always the reassuring 'messages from beyond the grave' through the spiritualist.

Like the claims of the serpent in Eden, these claims are hollow, empty, deceptive and can lead the 'occult explorer' into despair and destruction. What does the Bible say about such things?

> When you enter the land the LORD your God is giving you, do not learn to imitate the detestable ways of the nations there. Let no-one be found among you who sacrifices his son or daughter in the fire, who practises divination or sorcery, interprets omens, engages in witchcraft, or casts spells, or who is a medium or spiritist or who consults

the dead. Anyone who does these things is detestable to
the LORD, and because of these detestable practices the
LORD your God will drive out those nations before you.
You must be blameless before the LORD your God (Deut.
18:9–13).

This scripture alone shows that the claims of many
spiritualists to be 'Christian' are codswallop! Jesus said
that he was *The* Way, *The* Truth and *The* Life (see Jn. 14:6).
Assurance, safety and security in the face of difficulty are
not to be sought in manipulating dark powers but in a
relationship with him. 'I have come that they may have
life, and have it to the full' (Jn. 10:10b). 'For God so loved
the world that he gave his one and only Son, that whoever
believes in him shall not perish but have eternal life' (Jn.
3:16). 'I am the resurrection and the life. He who believes
in me will live, even though he dies; and whoever lives
and believes in me will never die' (Jn. 11:25–26).

These statements of Jesus reveal where the action
really is. Truth, direction and our eternal destiny are only
to be completely found in Jesus Christ. However, the ball
is in our court. We have the option to accept or reject his
offer of eternal life. We can live our lives God's way and
enjoying his blessing, or our own way and miss out. The
choice is ours.

The desire for fulfilment

One of the brilliant things about being a Christian is not
just that Christianity answers humanity's basic questions
like: 'Why am I here?' 'Who made me?' 'Who am I?' and
'What is my destiny?' but that we can actually, tangibly
experience God's love and power now in our lives, regardless of the situation. Millions upon millions of Christians
throughout history have proved this, both in the face of
poverty, torture, riot, persecution and death, as well as

during times of stability and peace with cash in hand and secure future prospects.

If there is one thing we can learn from a materialistic society, it is that money, success and happiness don't necessarily go hand in hand. We all secretly dream of success. A friend of mine says that anybody who hasn't put on a recording of the *1812 Overture* and conducted it with a ruler, or put a tea cosy on his head and pretended to be the Archbishop of Canterbury hasn't lived! I'd settle personally for mimicking the lead singer of Nickleback; my daughter, Christina Aguilera; and my son will act out scoring a hat trick for Newcastle United in the cup final!

As a teenager particularly, I remember that my prowess in playing lead guitar with the snooker cue was at its highest! However, at the age of nineteen when I became a Christian, I realised that for all the good music, success, gold discs and millions of dollars, many stars couldn't hold life together. They became enmeshed in alcoholism, drugs or, even worse, turned to the occult. Somehow the devotion of the crowds and the material prosperity were not enough. It is at this stage of disillusionment – feeling that there must be more to life than sexual expression and material success – that many turn for answers in some form of spiritual experience. In a spiritual vacuum many reach out and either find new life in Jesus Christ or begin flirting on the edge of the slippery slope into the occult. Just one harmless go on the Ouija board seems okay. But it's a step towards the slide into a dark abyss of fear.

I remember a fifteen-year-old girl coming to me after a school lesson I'd taken. She had been seeking spiritual fulfilment. A few turns of the tarot cards and having her fortune read led her into a literal nightmare of experiences. Every night for a year she had awoken paralysed with fear, hysterical and often violent and uncontrollable. Despite this she felt unable to throw the tarot cards away for fear of what these unseen forces would do to her. I told her about Jesus Christ and how he had broken Satan's power on the cross, making it possible for her to know God and be set free. After a short prayer session she became a Christian and was set free. That night she had her first period of uninterrupted sleep for a long time. Her mother, who was not a Christian, was so grateful that she took my wife and me out for a slap-up meal!

The occult is rather like drugs. It offers fulfilment for a short time, only to leave you hooked, not in control of your faculties but craving for more. The Bible, of course, recognises the need of humanity for fulfilment. To the woman of Samaria Jesus said: 'Everyone who drinks this water will be thirsty again, but whoever drinks the water I give him will never thirst. Indeed, the water I give him will become in him a spring of water welling up to eternal life' (Jn. 4:13, 14). (Please also read Jn. 4:7–25.)

The person who seeks fulfilment in Jesus Christ won't be disappointed. A relationship with God through him provides an endless supply of fulfilment – eternal life. Jesus said: 'The Spirit of the Lord is on me, because he has anointed me to preach good news to the poor. He has sent me to proclaim freedom for the prisoners and recovery of sight for the blind, to release the oppressed, to proclaim the year of the Lord's favour' (Lk. 4:18, 19).

Before I became a Christian, my philosophy was: 'Live now and pay later.' I looked at religion and churchianity which seemed to be saying: 'Pay now and live later.' Then I met Jesus and realised I could live now *and* live later. He became my hero.

The desire for adventure

Life can seem a bit boring sometimes with the same old routine and friends. The school holidays were great to start with, but by the end I was almost glad to get back to school.

Then I started work at the Civil Service. It made the school holidays seem like an exciting day trip to the moon, via Mars. Surely there had to be more to life than this?

I wanted to do something, be somebody, make something happen. Yet the odds seemed to be against me. Unemployment, competition for jobs, and it didn't help that I was as thick as two short planks. Surely there was somewhere I could find excitement and adventure?

It's when the odds seem stacked against us like this that many of us begin to look outside ourselves for another realm of experience. Many people drift into the occult this way. A friend of mine knocked on my door one day with five of his younger sister's friends, sixteen-year-old guys, cool, not prone to expose their emotions, but they looked awful.

'You look like you've seen a ghost,' I joked.

There were no laughs. Apparently, they had been bored and so one of them had the bright idea of playing with, you guessed it, a Ouija board. It started with jokes and laughs, but suddenly the atmosphere changed as the glass moved and questions were answered. Some of the answers were frightening, they were all afraid. One of the guys had developed an uncontrollable urge to commit suicide. They were not Christians, but knew that we were and wanted us to help.

I once read about a well-known TV programme that invited ordinary people, with a desire for adventure, to take part in potentially dangerous stunts. The highlight of the show every week was when the 'novice', under the direction of the professional, achieved a dramatic stunt. Unfortunately, on one occasion, the plans went tragically wrong. A young man plunged over a hundred feet to his death as a metal box he was in broke free from a crane.

We need to understand the difference between excitement, adventure, and Russian roulette. Believe the occult media blitz and you may find yourself with a revolver at your head. If you're lucky, it will be one of the five empty chambers. If you're not, your mind will be blown.

The Catalogue

Winter draws to a close, but it's still 'bloomin' parky' in our neck of the woods. Summer seems a million miles away in the mind of the average person, but sadistic TV presenters make us sit through tormenting horror shows about holidays. The contrast between Barbados and Bognor is almost too much for us to bear!

To make it worse, certain mail order firms decide to send us their summer catalogue. Why is it the free gifts are never as good as the picture portrays? The free luggage set which on the photo looks as large as a car boot turns out to be more like a handbag set. The shirt that makes the bloke in the photo look like Brad Pitt makes me look the pits! 'You can have it *now* for only £2.20 a week' ('for the next three years' in smaller print!). It always seems like they are virtually giving the stuff away, that is until the bill arrives.

If there was an occult catalogue, its index would run something like this: Astrology, Astral Travel, Automatic Writing, Divination, Freemasonry, Hallowe'en, Hallucinations, Horoscopes, Hypnotism, Levitation, Magic (Black and White), Mother Earth, Eastern Meditation and Mysticism, New Age, Ouija, Paganism, Psychic Powers, Reincarnation, Superstitions, Spiritualist Healing, Spiritualism, Tarot Cards, Table Tipping, Telepathy, Voodoo, Witchcraft, Yoga.

Packaged attractively, marketed efficiently, small print hidden from sight, these practices seem desirable. Normally we are encouraged to believe that they are either

Christian or, in contrast, not religious or spiritual at all. Membership is cheap, virtually free (again see the small print). No matter what you're into – sleeping around, drugs, lying, stealing – you can qualify immediately for occult membership. Just buy now and pay later. You may even be religious. Many people are fooled by this, and I've heard several accurate reports of so-called ministers and clergy being involved in spiritualism.

As we saw earlier, such things have nothing to do Christianity or Jesus Christ. The occult catalogue with its vast range of products is a convenient form of shopping for the modern religious seeker. Cheap membership and the absence of right and wrong mean that a little dabble here and there can hold the spiritual thirst at bay of people who find the claims and demands of Jesus Christ a little too taxing.

However, the personal cost of occult involvement can be great. Experience proves that we become whatever or whoever we serve. If we serve and worship dark powers we will become enslaved by the prince of darkness himself. If we serve money, the pursuit of it will master us, and if we serve God and live in his ways he will be our master. I know who *I'd* rather have as my boss – the loving, all-powerful God.

However, the gospel of Jesus Christ is not for the faint-hearted. Being a Christian is not being boring or religious, being born British, or attending church once a week. It involves making Jesus Christ number one in every area of your life. The prospect of this was too much for the rich young ruler (Mt. 19:16–22) who loved money more than God. He went away sad, unable to receive the good news.

The woman caught in adultery, however, reacted somewhat differently (Jn. 8:1–11). She was shamed and ostracised because of the wrong she had done and by the condemning, vicious attacks of the Pharisees who wanted to stone her, the penalty for adultery under Jewish law. She must have felt emotionally crippled, but Jesus offered her complete forgiveness and restoration with the proviso: 'Go now and leave your life of sin.'

The occult can offer us no forgiveness for sin, no cleansing of guilt, and will leave us wallowing helplessly in them both. Jesus Christ offers forgiveness, cleansing and the power of the Holy Spirit who enables us to live a changed life in victory over sin. 'Then Jesus said to his disciples, "If anyone would come after me, he must deny himself and take up his cross and follow me. For whoever wants to save his life will lose it, but whoever loses his life for me will find it"' (Mt. 16:24,25).

The Counterfeit

A young guy had recently become a Christian. As a teenager he was thrown out of his already broken home and had lived rough, getting involved in drugs and crime, as well as the occult. One day early in his Christian life he came to me with a confession: 'The police are after me.' Oh well, I thought, just a minor traffic offence or something. He paused, took a deep breath and pulled out a wad of £20 notes from his pockets.

'You've nicked them I suppose,' I exclaimed.

'Oh no, I wouldn't do that,' he said. 'They're counterfeit.'

I nearly fell off my chair! He had obtained these notes and had been around town buying presents and treating his unknowing friends to slap-up meals. Suddenly, while he was sitting with some people from church in a restaurant, he had without warning run off, leaving them with the bill, the Old Bill and a lot of explaining to do! After a few words and some prayer, my young friend had decided to accompany me to the station, and was eventually released under my care after a full confession. Fortunately for him, when his case made court he escaped a prison sentence but he was still given a hefty fine, probation and lengthy community service.

The occult is rather like that counterfeit money. It is not the real thing, but it looks like it. It appears to promise some of the products of real spirituality, such as happiness and peace. But in the end, time runs out, the goods have to be handed back, and a penalty has to be paid. Things were not as they seemed. Satan the deceiver had been at work.

Jesus Christ said: 'I am the way and the truth and the life' (Jn. 14:6). True spirituality is only to be found in him.

Chapter 2

From Atheism to New Age

'Get your 3D glasses here!' exclaimed the 6-foot Disney employee who was modelling the latest Donald Duck costume as the Ellis family moved with the long queue into the 'Bugs and Spiders' show. With the glasses on, the screen came alive. Spiders, bugs and all kinds of creepy crawlies appeared to come right over to us. Couple this with moving chairs, breezes and all sorts of other effects and the Ellis family were screaming wrecks.

Lenses certainly affect the way we see things. Sunglasses are another phenomenon. Come spring and summer everybody is wearing them. As a keen fisherman, I wouldn't dream of going fishing without mine. Surface glare on the water means that without sunglasses it is virtually impossible to see those big, fat, slimy carp feeding away on the lake bottom. I've seen fishermen, without sunglasses, walk straight past a whole group of feeding fish and begin fishing in an area which is totally devoid of them, leaving me to capitalise on the opportunity of a big catch. However, sunglasses are only useful during the day, and at night they can be a positive hindrance.

Clearly the lens through which we view life will influence the conclusions we make on any subject. Our world-view is all-important. It will either help us understand truth and come to a knowledge of God, or keep us in ignorance. The person with an atheistic view will presuppose quite categorically that there is absolutely no chance of there being a God. Like the fisherman without the sunglasses, he will walk around in life blissfully unaware of all the spiritual activity going on under the surface. Any evidence for God's existence that emerges is filed away, dismissed or put into the mystery bracket. As Gerald Coates observes: 'If God was to poke his head round the corner and say "Boo!" many atheists would spend the rest of their lives trying to explain why it wasn't God.'[1]

The agnostic, who is not sure whether there is a God or not, will hear about the 3D glasses (experience of God) and see others wearing them, but until he tries a pair for himself he will remain in uncertainty.

What I want to do in this chapter is to look at some of the different world-views that affect our society today and see how these influence our understanding of the occult.

An Atheist's World-View

The graffiti on the subway wall read: *God is dead – Nietzsche.* Some enterprising person had added alongside: *Nietzsche is dead – God!* Many atheist philosophers have boldly declared that science has disproved God's existence. However, the theory of evolution and the 'big bang' theory remain just that – theories! One of the things evolutionists often forget about the missing link (a life form between monkey and human that would prove our evolution from apes) is that it is still just that – missing! Even if we subscribe to the 'big bang' theory we are left with a problem: 'Who made the

---

[1] Quote from a talk by Gerald that I heard in the 1980s.

big bang?' As one leading non-Christian scientist said, 'To believe that the big bang created life is rather like believing that an explosion in a junk yard gave birth to Concorde!'

It seems to me that you need more faith to remain an atheist than to believe in Creator God these days. However, many intelligent people hold this position, and to remain consistent with their world-view they would have to relegate any belief in the occult or God to the realm of pure fantasy. From my perspective as a Christian, believing in both God and the devil, I can see how clever the powers of darkness are.

One of the devil's names in Scripture is Satan which means the adversary or enemy of both God and humanity. His attacks are rarely out-and-out but more like guerrilla warfare. What better place to be as an enemy power, than to have the opposite side not even believing you exist! You can be free to operate without any resistance.

One area that has been particularly prone to enemy attack is the whole area of morality, or right and wrong. Christian moral absolutes are not based on human inventions, but on what God himself is like.

The commandment 'You shall not commit adultery' (Ex. 20:14) does not come from the fact that God has decided adultery is bad news (though he has), but that adultery or unfaithfulness are totally alien to his character. God is a God of absolute faithfulness; we can trust him totally. The greatest commandment, to 'Love the Lord your God with all your heart and with all your soul and with all your mind and with all your strength', is followed by the command to 'Love your neighbour as yourself' (see Mk. 12:28–31). This is based on the character of God himself, for 'God is love' (1 Jn. 4:16).

By contrast, the atheist has no supreme being to draw moral absolutes from. I was talking to an atheist about sexual morality and he was speaking against one-partner-only relationships saying, 'We are just another animal. Why can't we be like dogs that mate with whatever dog they feel like, whenever they want?' My reply was, firstly, that humans are more than animals, and secondly, that if that was the case he wouldn't mind finding his wife in bed with the milkman when he arrived home. He looked at me somewhat surprised and said, 'Oh no, that would be different!' Apparently, in his book, adultery can't be termed absolutely wrong unless of course he fell victim to it personally! Not believing in God, atheists have to play God and make up what's right and wrong as they go along.

We then have a morality of means. We do whatever seems right at the time. The extreme fruit of a morality of means could be seen in the horrific extermination of six million Jews by Hitler's regime in the Second World War. Within Hitler's twisted, godless 'morality' it was perfectly all right to murder all those innocent people. Humanity without God is prone to satanically influenced morality.

In the Bible Satan is called 'a murderer from the beginning' (Jn. 8:44). It is not hard to see therefore who was at work behind the holocaust. The atheist must declare himself 'God' and reason away any and every supernatural event that has ever or will ever occur. In his mind, all the millions of people who have been sustained by their faith in God and died still believing must be sincerely deluded.

An Eastern or Monist's World-View

Have you ever found yourself talking at cross-purposes with someone because you both have a different understanding of a particular word? I remember talking for a few minutes to an American about football. We both agreed what a great sport it was, possibly the best of all, only to find out that I was talking about English soccer and he, American football. Instead of agreeing, we ended up disagreeing!

Similarly, in other countries, some habits have different meanings than they have in Britain. For instance, if I were to let out a loud burp after a nice meal which my wife had cooked she wouldn't be very pleased. However, in certain Arab countries, it is considered a compliment to your host to burp heartily after a slap-up meal. It is a sign of appreciation.

When talking about God to Eastern thinkers, the Christian is very likely to end up in a similar dilemma because their concept of God is totally at odds with our own. Most would not see God as a personal, distinct being separate to and apart from creation, as Christians would. Rather god (with a small 'g' for them and a big 'G' for us) is reality, energy and life force. All is god, animal, mineral, tree, fish, animate and inanimate. The presence of god can be worshipped in everything: cows, cats, various animals; anything and everything has god in it. The ordinary Hindu may worship any of a multitude of different gods.

This concept of God is totally alien to the Judeo-Christian world-view which firmly says that no created thing, be it heavenly or earthly, is to be worshipped (Ex. 20:4). Such worship is seen by the Bible as vain and foolish (Rom. 1:21–23).

Many religious people like to say that 'all roads lead to God'. This is impossible as the god that the Hindus and many Eastern cults are trying to get to is not a person like the God of the Christian. And with regard to Buddhism, there is no god as such. These religions compared with Christianity are like chalk and cheese.

Eastern Philosophy

'What's that?' you may ask. 'Is it catching?' Well, it may be!

The Eastern thinker not only believes that there are no absolutes: no right and no wrong, no good and no bad – he also believes that there is no this or that. This would particularly apply within Buddhism. Good and evil are just different ends of the same reality, just like male and female represent different aspects of one humanity. When you believe there is no right or wrong, and that animals and humans both have 'godness' in them, it is not hard to go to the extremes that some animal rights protesters have in endangering or harming human life in order to preserve animals because they believe animals and humans are equal. (This is not to say that we as humans should not stand against animal exploitation, however.) In fact these beliefs don't just deny the personality of God, but they deny all separate personality, believing that we are all one with the cosmos.

In fact the Eastern thinker, because of his belief that there is no this or that, cannot be sure of what is reality. 'What is existence? Which is the dream?' he may well ask. 'How do I know that what I am now is not a dream, and the dream I had last night is not reality?' I may dream that I have inherited a million pounds, but unfortunately the statement I receive from my bank the next day will not show money credited to my account! My dream was not reality in the cold light of day.

The Bible is clear that God is a distinct personal being and so are all humans. We have been given life by God himself and one day every person will give an account to him for the way he has lived.

Let us briefly, and therefore inadequately, explore some other terms that would leave Christians at cross purposes with many who have this Eastern world-view.

Sin (or wrongdoing) and salvation

To the Christian the word 'sin' is not just a cliché. In the biblical Greek language it was an archery term meaning 'to miss the mark' (bull's eye). Anything short of perfection, namely the perfect character of God himself, is sin. Now we can see why the Bible says that 'all have sinned and fall short of the glory of God' (Rom. 3:23). Humanity's imperfections build a barrier between us and God, preventing us from sharing a relationship with him.

However, we need not retreat in fear or despair because Jesus Christ has provided the way for us to have our relationship with God restored. This is part of the meaning of the word 'salvation'.

> If we claim to be without sin, we deceive ourselves and the truth is not in us. If we confess our sins, he is faithful and just and will forgive us our sins and purify us from all unrighteousness (1 Jn. 1:8, 9).

> For the wages of sin is death, but the gift of God is eternal life in Christ Jesus our Lord (Rom. 6:23).

To some Hindus, sin simply does not exist as there can be no barrier between God and humanity (we are all gods). To these Hindus sin is maya (illusion), or the failure to recognise reality or see through the maya. Reality is the Universal Soul (nothingness). Salvation for the Hindu is not seen as having a relationship with the living God, but is a process of enlightenment and realisation during which we must rid our consciousness of all reason. Salvation is ultimate reality, Brahman, or absolute nothingness. The equation goes something like this: *Reality = nothing. Salvation = absolute reality = absolute nothing.* If there is any sin at all it consists of the failure to recognise absolutely nothing when you see it. It all makes perfect sense!

Good and evil/Satan

As we have said, to the Eastern or monistic mind all is one. Nothing is absolutely good or absolutely evil. Good and evil permeate each other. This is particularly true within the Chinese religion, Taoism. A Taoist would find it very hard to relate to the God of the Christian, who is absolute perfection. Within this confusion, any type of moral or religious practice seems to be okay. Spiritualism, witchcraft, divination, ancestor worship, the casting of spells, cursing, as well as astrology abound. You can see why, in order to understand the wide range of occult influence in society today, we must first get to grips with this particular world-view. We will see more of this in Chapter 5. All that really needs to be said at this stage is that the monistic or Eastern world-view is taking much ground in society today.

The New Age Movement, with its emphasis on reincarnation, yoga and other practices, has brought a new awareness of the supernatural to the West. Maintaining either that it is not religious, or conversely even masquerading as Christian, New Age cults like Scientology (dianetics, gathering well-known followers like Tom Cruise), transcendental meditation (TM) and many others have drawn thousands of people into their web of influence. Even atheists and agnostics have been drawn in, having been sold the lie that meditation and yoga are not spiritual but to do with energy and the development of your human potential.

To the Eastern mind, the life of 'god' is seen only in one context – 'holistic' or the term monism/oneism. The Taoist or Zen Buddhist sees that in everything good there is something bad and in everything bad there is something good. Together they (good and bad) make up one being which includes god, humanity and everything;

Taoism: Good and Evil

the conclusion being that evil is part of the inherent nature of God. Well-known Buddhists include Keanu Reeves of *The Matrix* fame.

As we will see later, yoga, both in Hinduism (its source) and the West, has to do with provoking spirit reactions through physical positions. A friend of mine who was a Hindu and has now become a Christian says, 'To the Hindu, yoga and meditation are always religious and cannot be separated from worship.' The innocent person taking part in exercise therapies may, if he is not careful, end up involved in the occult. The Eastern or monistic world-view is a doorway into a spiritual awareness that the Bible would declare both dangerous and foolish.

Specifically speaking
While my general statements may be a helpful introduction to Eastern thought, I will now briefly differentiate between the various forms of Hinduism, Buddhism and Taoism.

Basically there are two sorts of Hinduism:

1. *'Non-dualist'* or *'advaita'*. It is in this form that there is no personal God, only the absolute or Brahman. Everything is Brahman (as opposed to god being in everything, which is pantheism). There is no this or that: all is one. The aim is to realise that we are all Brahman, or god, because Brahman is everything. Therefore prayer and worship is pointless. After all, you are only talking to yourself!

2. *Bhakti (meaning devotion)*. Brahman is worshipped through the god Vishnu, who is reincarnated in many people, including Krishna. Other reincarnations (*avatars*) of Brahman are supposed to include recent modern-day gurus like Rajneesh and the Maharishi Mahesh Yogi. Gurus are worshipped along with many idol forms and much superstition.

Buddhism, by contrast, represents a reaction against Hinduism.

Buddha was originally a Hindu but maintained that Hinduism didn't go far enough. The Hindu says that everything is Brahman, but the Buddhist would go further, saying everything is 'nothing'. The aim of the Buddhist is to attain *nirvana* or *sunyata* (the void or vacuum). Once we realise we don't exist we sink into the void of nothingness.

Alongside this there are three forms of Buddhism:

1. *Non-being or Theravada*. This is particularly found in Thailand, Sri Lanka and Laos. The aim of Theravada is to reach the void or *nirvana*.

2. *Mahayana Buddhism*. This is particularly found in China, Japan and Korea. It would basically assert that we all have the Buddha spirit within and that

by means of a good life and meditation we can be realised and in turn become a Buddha.

3. *Zen Buddhism*. 'Ducks have short legs, cranes long legs', or so goes a famous Zen saying. You may be evil; I may be good. We cannot help it and there is nothing we can do to change. We must accept it. Enlightenment comes through total acceptance and no more striving for anything.

Buddhists believe that all existence is suffering and that the cause of suffering is thirst or desire. Desire covers not just negative passions (like lust and anger) but includes all emotions, like love and joy. Therefore all desire is evil. The cause of desire is the fact that we exist, and therefore we must get rid of all existence and emotion. When we have done this there will be no suffering because there is no existence. Hence, the aim of the Zen Buddhist is *sunyata*, the void of nothingness.

Syncretism

Another factor to take into account is syncretism. Sounds painful, you may think. Well, it can be!

Basically, syncretism is where different faiths are merged together and begin to lose their individual distinctiveness. Within Eastern religion, and particularly the New Age Movement, this often happens. You find that the beliefs of Hinduism, Buddhism and Taoism become intertwined. Therefore, it is not unusual to see strong elements of both Hinduism and Buddhism muddled together in much New Age thinking. At the same time, within Hinduism there are monotheists (believing in one god), polytheists (believing in many gods), pantheists (god is in everything) and animists (ancestor worship). Quite a mixture!

A Christian World-View

Atheists, by nature of their standpoint, are making a bold assertion about God's non-existence. They are saying by inference that they have searched all the evidence in heaven and on earth and can state categorically that there is definitely no God. Most people could not in all honesty make that statement and would therefore fall into the agnostic or 'don't know' bracket.

As a Christian, my assertion is somewhat different. Within the evidence I've surveyed, which is only a small part of that which is available, I have never discovered anything – either intellectually or experientially – that has disproved my Christian faith. On the contrary, the evidence available was instrumental in my conversion to Christianity and the subsequent strengthening of my faith. This is not to say that I or anybody else has all the answers, but I have enough answers to satisfy my curiosity, base my faith on and provoke me to want to explore more.

The Christian world-view sees the person of God as Boss over all things. He has always existed, exists now, and always will exist. Quite a concept for us mere earthlings to handle. Next summer often seems a long way away, never mind eternity. God's ways are higher than our ways, and his thoughts higher than our thoughts (Is. 55:9). It is impossible for us as created beings to understand everything about the God who created everything. However, we *can* know him.

Critical problems

Any critic with an ounce of common sense is liable to come up with at least two questions at this point.

1. How can you believe in a perfect God of love when there is so much suffering in the world? Any God who created suffering must be a monster.

2. How can you believe in the devil, demons and the supernatural in this day and age? Surely we grew out of this in the Middle Ages?

Some answers

1. I approach the problem of suffering knowing I can never do the subject justice in this limited space with my limited brainpower. I am also aware that while the Bible offers reasons for suffering and hope in the face of it, suffering will always be one of life's great mysteries and dilemmas. Trite answers are to be avoided at all costs.

Having said that, I would agree with the questioner. Any God who created suffering and good and evil must be at best a 'schizo', and at worst deranged. However, nowhere in the Bible does it say that God created suffering. The story of Creation, whilst not being a scientific declaration of the how, explains to us the 'why' and 'what happened'.

Genesis declares that everything God made was perfect. He pronounced it 'very good' (Gen. 1:31). It is clear that both man and woman were having a whale of a time. It was literally paradise. They were in charge of things on God's behalf. Not a bad job really.

The animals were not fierce but friendly, the earth yielded its produce easily, natural disasters like earthquakes and famines did not exist. Words like 'death', 'pain' and 'evil' were not in their vocabulary. All this was for humanity to enjoy, with one proviso: '. . . you must not eat from the tree of the knowledge of good and evil, for when you eat of it you will surely die' (Gen. 2:17). They had freedom to choose, but the choice to rebel against God would affect humanity and creation completely. We would be subject to physical death (at that time humanity had eternal life) and lose our relationship with God.

Well, the rest is history. Humanity listened to the serpent (enter Satan) rather than God, and as a result we fell from God's presence (Genesis 3). Creation fell, bringing all sickness and suffering, death, disaster and evil into our experience. Our rebellion cost us deeply, but was also to cost God the ultimate price to save us from our self-inflicted predicament. The price was his only Son, Jesus Christ.

> Who, being in very nature God, did not consider equality with God something to be grasped, but made himself nothing, taking the very nature of a servant, being made in human likeness. And being found in appearance as a man, he humbled himself and became obedient to death – even death on a cross! (Phil. 2:6–8)

> To this you were called, because Christ suffered for you, leaving you an example, that you should follow in his steps. 'He committed no sin, and no deceit was found in his mouth.' When they hurled their insults at him, he did not retaliate; when he suffered, he made no threats. Instead, he entrusted himself to him who judges justly. He himself bore our sins in his body on the tree, so that we might die to sins and live for righteousness; by his wounds you have been healed. For you were like sheep going astray, but now you have returned to the Shepherd and Overseer of your souls (1 Pet. 2:21–25).

The suffering in this world has no origin in God, but in humanity's rebellion against God.

2.   There are actually some Christians around who find it hard to believe the devil exists (as well as non-Christians, of course). Looking at the evil in the world, it seems logical to me that if there is a God as the source of good (and

there is), then there must also be a devil. The existence of evil demands the existence of an evil source (Satan). It is impossible to make sense of things otherwise.

Of course, the Bible is full of teaching on Satan. It answers such questions as: 'Who is he?' 'Who made him?' and 'What is his destiny?' as we will see in later chapters as we deal more specifically with the occult. Despite developments in science, medicine and the dawn of the computer age, we are in a society where belief in the supernatural is on the increase. This will give us as Christians many opportunities to share about our faith in Jesus Christ. On the flip side, however, this spiritual vacuum will mean the growth of many occult movements in this country.

Fortunately as Christians we can have a clear perspective on both good and evil. We have a friendship with the all-powerful God through Jesus and have been rescued from the kingdom of darkness into God's kingdom (Col. 1:13). We are not without hope like the atheist, in ignorance like the agnostic, and neither are we subject to the confusion of the Eastern thinker or monist. We have a relationship with the living God and know there is more to life than meets the eye (Eph. 6:10–12).

Chapter 3

Who is the Boss?
Occult Power – The Great Rip-Off

I remember at the age of nineteen, having been convinced of my belief in God and the supernatural, weighing up what I wanted to do with my life. God and the devil existed. Jesus Christ, God himself, had died an agonising death on my behalf, and to cap it all he'd risen from the dead, offering me a new life following him. I had been happy enough I suppose, but the prospect of an exciting life serving God seemed irresistible. Even the cost of handing my whole life to him seemed miniscule compared to what Jesus had done for me. I could see why the disciples instantly snapped up their opportunity to follow Jesus (Mt. 4:18–22). It seemed a risk, but that somehow made it even more attractive. Anyway, how could I lose? God was God and Jesus Christ had emerged victorious from every situation, even death itself. Everybody likes to be on the winning side; I figured that not even I could go wrong with God.

> Who shall separate us from the love of Christ? Shall trouble or hardship or persecution or famine or nakedness or danger or sword? As it is written: 'For your sake we face death all day long; we are considered as sheep to be slaughtered.' No, in all these things we are more

than conquerors through him who loved us. For I am
convinced that neither death nor life, neither angels
nor demons, neither the present nor the future, nor any
powers, neither height nor depth, nor anything else in all
creation, will be able to separate us from the love of God
that is in Christ Jesus our Lord (Rom. 8:35–39).

If I was going to invest my life in anyone he seemed by
far the best bet!

Thinking this way, I have never quite been able to
understand people who become involved in the occult
– despite the surface attractions we saw in Chapter 1. It is
clear from the Bible that God is the Boss and that occult
devotees are enslaving themselves to a defeated power
who is at present on a long leash. Satan in fact owes his
whole existence to Creator God. He is a created being and
as a result only has the power and authority allowed by
God within the created order.

We are now going to look at some Bible passages that
reveal this created order of authority. These show that God
has put Satan firmly in his place and given Christians real
authority in Jesus by which we can overcome the powers
of darkness. The devil is the great door-to-door trickster,
using deception to convince many of his followers that
he holds the answers. In actual fact, a warrant is out for
his arrest, his fate has been sealed and his days have been
numbered by God himself.

The Created Order

When I consider your heavens, the work of your fingers,
the moon and the stars, which you have set in place, what
is man that you are mindful of him, the son of man that
you care for him? You made him a little lower than the
heavenly beings and crowned him with glory and honour.

You made him ruler over the works of your hands; you put everything under his feet: all flocks and herds, and the beasts of the field, the birds of the air, and the fish of the sea, all that swim the paths of the seas (Ps. 8:3–9 – see also Heb. 2:6–8).

1. *Hebrews 2:7 – Creation*
Hebrews: *angelos* = angels
GOD (Father, Son and Holy Spirit)
ANGELS (including Satan)
HUMANITY
ANIMALS

2. *Ephesians 1:19–23 – Birth, death and resurrection of Jesus Christ*
GOD (the Father)
JESUS CHRIST
ANGELS (including Satan)
HUMANITY
ANIMALS

3. *Ephesians 2:4–7 – Our position as Christians in Christ*
GOD
JESUS CHRIST
HUMANITY WITH JESUS (those 'in Christ')
ANGELS (including Satan)
HUMANITY WITHOUT JESUS
ANIMALS

We have authority *in Christ* over all the powers of darkness. A legal position over Satan.

4. *NB*
ANGELS (spiritual beings)
HUMANITY (spiritual and physical beings in the image of God)
ANIMALS (physical beings)

Humanity is unique and special in all creation. Humanity is distinct from the animal realm, but is called to care responsibly for it.[2]

God

As you can see from part one of the created order, God set in place a definite order of authority at creation. He did not make a world that was in anarchy with many different forces at war, struggling with one another in distress and disorder, just like a riot. Rather, there was a definite order within which every aspect of creation could operate in harmony.

Angels

God created an angelic realm which included Satan (we'll see more of this later). These powerful spirit beings had the inbuilt ability to relate to God himself who is spirit (Jn. 4:24).

Humanity

Underneath the angels God created human beings who were both spiritual and physical. Human beings had the ability to relate freely to God (until they rebelled against him that is), but could also maintain the earth on his behalf physically. Man and woman were unique in all creation.

> So God created man in his own image, in the image of God he created him; male and female he created them. God blessed them and said to them, 'Be fruitful and increase in number; fill the earth and subdue it. Rule over the fish of the sea and the birds of the air and over every living creature that moves on the ground' (Gen. 1:27, 28).

---

[2] The created order idea taken from Roger Price, *Victory in Jesus*, Marshall, Morgan & Scott, 1982 – now out of print.

Made in the image and likeness of God himself, they had an honour not bestowed upon the animal kingdom. Perhaps this image can be partly understood in the following ways.

1. The ability to think things out based on the intellect. The ability to use detailed communication.

2. Self-awareness and consciousness. Conscience; the presence in one form or another of the sense of right and wrong. The ability to make free moral choices.

3. The ability to love, and to make decisions and to have a sense of humour.

4. Superiority over nature. Creative instincts.

5. The ability to know God and to relate to him.

All this points to the fact that humanity is in some strange way a reflection of God. The likeness of his Creator is in some special way present, over and above any other part of creation. Humanity is a 'chip off the old block'.

Animals

As part of creation, animals are vital and precious. Humanity needs once again to take its God-given responsibility for the animals and creation seriously. Christians have biblical backing behind them when they speak on issues of environmental pollution and animal conservation. However, nowhere in the Bible does it suggest that animals reflect the image of God in the same way that humans do. Since they are only physical beings, the answer to the question 'Does my budgie need to be saved?' is therefore 'No'!

We saw in Chapter 1 that when humanity fell away from God, creation fell with him. By this I mean that the book of Genesis links humanity's first sin on the earth to the emergence of earthquakes, famine and natural disasters. Before this event, creation was in total perfection and harmony. Well, in the same way that the first sin of humanity is linked with the suffering in creation, so the salvation of humanity is linked to the rescue of all creation.

Jesus Christ Changes Things

When Jesus Christ was born it caused quite a stir! Angels announced his arrival in advance. Wise men visited him after his birth, acknowledging his kingship. This put the wind up Herod, the king at the time, who ordered every child under the age of two years to be put to death (Mt. 2).

Jesus' public life was equally as eventful. The sick were healed and the dead raised, and thousands of people trooped into remote areas to hear his remarkable teaching. He even arranged a miraculous spur-of-the-moment banquet for five thousand of them (Mk. 6:30–44). Not even McDonalds fast food could be that fast! The effect of those remarkable events was nothing compared to the effect that the power of his death and resurrection has had on the earth for all time. Christians maintain that this is the centre-point of all history. After all, time itself is measured by Christian and non-Christian alike with regard to the life of Jesus Christ. For instance, archaeologists would date the Exodus of the Jews from Egypt (see the book of Exodus) under Rameses II at between 1290 and 1224 BC (before Christ). Later events like the Battle of Hastings have been recorded as AD 1066 (after Christ). However, the death and resurrection of Jesus did more than affect our diaries. We saw in Chapter 2 that through this event eternal life could be given back to humanity: specifically and personally to those who would give their lives back to God. If that's not enough, the whole created order is being changed.

> I pray also that the eyes of your heart may be enlightened in order that you may know the hope to which he has called you, the riches of his glorious inheritance in the saints, and his incomparably great power for us who believe. That power is like the working of his mighty strength, which he exerted in Christ when he raised him from the dead and seated him at his right hand in the heavenly realms, far above all rule and authority, power and dominion, and every title that can be given, not only in the present age but also in the one to come. And God placed all things under his feet and appointed him to be head over everything for the church, which is his body, the fullness of him who fills everything in every way (Eph. 1:18–23).

(See part 2 of the created order.)

Jesus came to earth as perfect God and perfect Man and through his life, death and resurrection he proved he was the Boss.

> Who, being in very nature God, did not consider equality with God something to be grasped, but made himself nothing, taking the very nature of a servant, being made in human likeness. And being found in appearance as a man, he humbled himself and became obedient to death – even death on a cross! Therefore God exalted him to the highest place and gave him the name that is above every name, that at the name of Jesus every knee should bow, in heaven and on earth and under the earth, and every tongue confess that Jesus Christ is Lord, to the glory of God the Father (Phil. 2:6–11).

Jesus Christ sits at the right hand of God the Father. The 'right hand' simply means the place of all authority, power and rulership. We'd better believe it! At the moment, we have the choice whether or not to recognise this, but this will not always be so. One day, after death or when Jesus comes again, even those who reject him now will have to submit to his authority. Not to his love, as Christians will, but to judgement. When you're on God's side you are safe. Outside of God there are no guarantees; Russian roulette all over again.

How Does This Affect Christians?

> But because of his great love for us, God, who is rich in mercy, made us alive with Christ even when we were dead in transgressions – it is by grace you have been saved. And God raised us up with Christ and seated us with him in the heavenly realms in Christ Jesus, in order that in the coming ages he might show the incomparable riches of his grace, expressed in his kindness to us in Christ Jesus. For it is by grace you have been saved, through faith – and this not from yourselves, it is the gift of God – not by works, so that no-one can boast (Eph. 2:4–9).

(See part 3 of the created order.)

It's amazing what a position of authority does for a person. The appointed captain of a sports team has no authority suddenly to begin conducting traffic during his lunch hour. He's liable to be flattened by an oncoming lorry! Only the police have authority to direct traffic. However, when it comes to picking the team, selecting a strategy and barking orders during the game, the captain is the boss.

Part 3 of the created order shows us that Christians have been given position *in Christ*. This doesn't mean that we are any better than other people (Eph. 2:8, 9), but that God has appointed us in Christ to this position. We therefore have spiritual authority over the angelic realm, particularly Satan and the powers of the occult.

Some of the early disciples found this out when Jesus sent them to proclaim the good news of the kingdom of God to people who had never heard it.

> The seventy-two returned with joy and said, 'Lord, even the demons submit to us in your name.' He replied, 'I saw Satan fall like lightning from heaven. I have given you authority to trample on snakes and scorpions and to overcome all the power of the enemy; nothing will harm you. However, do not rejoice that the spirits submit to you, but rejoice that your names are written in heaven' (Lk. 10:17–20).

Before we go on to consider the occult, as Christians we need firstly to understand and get hold of our authority and victory in Jesus. Secondly, we need to know the strengths and weaknesses of our enemy.

Know Your Enemy

There are two grave mistakes that a commander could make when battling against an enemy force. Firstly, he could over-estimate his enemy's firepower and retreat fearfully, fighting a defensive battle. This means that he could give land over unnecessarily to enemy occupation. Secondly, he could underestimate the enemy's power. To take the battle result for granted and treat the enemy with contempt means that he could be in for a nasty surprise.

Many Christians box shy of spiritual warfare, afraid of the powers of darkness and unaware of the authority they have in Jesus. No wonder occult involvement continues to mushroom when Christians are too wet to stand up in the power of the Holy Spirit.

On the other hand, we must engage in spiritual warfare carefully. I remember one of the first people I prayed for with an occult-related problem. He had severe suicidal and destructive tendencies. My friend and I closed our eyes and prayed somewhat nonchalantly for the spirit of destruction to leave him. I've learnt since never to close my eyes during such prayer, for when I opened them I was confronted with a horrible sight. The person's face had totally contorted and he was attempting to strangle himself, gouge his eyes out and have a go at us! Naturally frightened, I moved up a gear and commanded the spirit to leave him in the name of Jesus. He was released and none the worse for his experience. I had learnt my lesson.

A summary

We are now going to summarise the Bible's teaching on the devil. Who is he? Where does he come from? What is his destiny? We shall start by looking at the Old Testament prophecies which will throw some light on this particular subject.

> The word of the LORD came to me: 'Son of man, take up a lament concerning the king of Tyre and say to him: "This is what the Sovereign LORD says: 'You were the model of perfection, full of wisdom and perfect in beauty. You were in Eden, the garden of God; every precious stone adorned you: ruby, topaz and emerald, chrysolite, onyx and jasper, sapphire, turquoise and beryl. Your settings and mountings were made gold; on the day you were created they were prepared. You were anointed as a guardian cherub, for so I ordained you. You were on the holy mount of God; you walked among the fiery stones. You were blameless in your ways from the day you were created till wickedness was found in you. Through your widespread trade you were filled with violence, and you sinned. So I drove you in disgrace from the mount of

God, and I expelled you, O guardian cherub, from among the fiery stones. Your heart became proud on account of your beauty, and you corrupted your wisdom because of your splendour. So I threw you to the earth; I made a spectacle of you before kings. By your many sins and dishonest trade you have desecrated your sanctuaries. So I made a fire come out from you, and it consumed you, and I reduced you to ashes on the ground in the sight of all who were watching. All the nations who knew you are appalled at you; you have come to a horrible end and will be no more'"' (Ezek. 28:11–19).

All your pomp has been brought down to the grave, along with the noise of your harps; maggots are spread out beneath you and worms cover you. How you have fallen from heaven, O morning star, son of the dawn! You have been cast down to the earth, you who once laid low the nations! You said in your heart, 'I will ascend to heaven; I will raise my throne above the stars of God; I will sit enthroned on the mount of assembly, on the utmost heights of the sacred mountain. I will ascend above the tops of the clouds; I will make myself like the Most High' But you are brought down to the grave, to the depths of the pit (Is. 14:11–15).

I remember when I first started to read the Old Testament, these passages seemed like double Dutch to me. I soon learnt not to be daunted by them, and some background reading gave me the gist of what was being said.

Some ground rules

All Old Testament passages have a historical context, but behind this the prophet is often referring to a spiritual reality or prophesying a future event. Take for example Psalm 22. David starts by saying, 'My God, my God, why have you forsaken me?' and then goes on to bemoan his persecution at the hand of his enemies. The next minute, however, he is prophesying and in verses 14–18 describes crucifixion (remarkable, since it didn't exist in his day). This wasn't any ordinary crucifixion either.

It was the death of the Messiah, Jesus Christ, described right down to the casting of lots for his clothes (compare Ps. 22:18 with Mk. 15:24). Incredible, unbelievable, but such is the power of the Bible.

Going back to our passages in Ezekiel and Isaiah, we can see that the prophets talked of more than immediate circumstances. Since when had the king of Tyre been in the Garden of Eden as a guardian angel (Ezek. 28:13,14)? He certainly wasn't an angel – or at least we have no record of him having wings! He'd also have had to have been knocking on a bit to have lived from Eden to Ezekiel's time! Neither, for that matter, did the King of Babylon try to ascend to heaven above God (Is. 14:11–13). Obviously there is more to these passages than initially meets the eye. They tell of the creation, fall and judgement of Satan.

Seven things every Christian should know about the devil

1. *He is not eternal or self-existent.* He is a created being just like us. He owes his existence and ongoing life to God. Any power he has in himself was given to him when he was created. He owes it all to God and therefore there is not an equal battle between 'good and evil' (called dualism by some) but God as Creator is Boss.

2. *He is a fallen angel.* Satan was a guardian cherub – an angel similar in authority to the archangel Michael (Dan. 10:13, Jude 9). He staged a revolution against God at some point prior to the fall of humanity. In pride he tried to overthrow God's power and as a result was thrown from heaven. In this fall, all of his former angelic beauty was thoroughly corrupted,

twisted and polluted. He is now totally evil. Satan cannot be saved from his fall as humanity can. His judgement is sealed and his destruction date set by God (Rev. 20:10).

3. *His power operates within God's boundaries (sovereignty).* God is King. All of creation is subject to him to the degree that when Satan wanted to attack Job he had to first seek God's permission (Job 1:6–12).

4. *God's forces are superior.* It's really good to know that as Christians we can be totally secure in God. In fact God is so powerful he is able to use Satan for his own ends. There are biblical illustrations of this, such as the crucifixion, but I'll give you a personal example. My friend Malcolm, before becoming a Christian, had heard about God quite a few times from another friend of mine, also called Malcolm, at work. He didn't do anything about it because he didn't fancy the cost of becoming a Christian. One weekend he was at another friend's house (who has since become a Christian) whose mother was into the occult. She offered to practise tarot cards and pendulum swinging on his behalf. He had a terrible experience of fear and panic! Satan had overstepped the mark. Malcolm's experience of the occult, a totally bad thing, was used by God to enable him to take the step and become a Christian.

5. *He's not all-knowing.* God has the benefit of complete knowledge, but the devil doesn't. If he did, he would have tried to prevent Jesus dying on the cross instead of provoking it. The cross which seemed to be a great defeat for God became his greatest victory.

6. *He can't be everywhere at the same time.* When Satan fell from heaven he took a minority proportion of

the angels with him (demons). He is not able to work in all places personally, but relies on the work of demons. God, by contrast, can be everywhere by his Holy Spirit and has a whole stack of angels at his disposal too.

7. *He's not all-powerful.* His power is limited by God's unlimited power.

A Kingdom of Evil?

Imagine a multinational corporation with worldwide operations worth billions of dollars, ranging from oil interests in the Middle East, agriculture in the States, mining in South Africa and a large microchip division in both America and Britain. Such corporations exist and they have tremendous power. Some of them have more cash at their disposal than an entire national government. In order to maintain the running of the corporation efficiently, keeping profits at the highest level, the overall strategy must be linked. Smooth-running leadership is essential with strong, powerful authority. It's 'dog eat dog' to get to the top. The power threat of the boss ensures that management at world, national, local and individual levels runs like a well-oiled machine.

The Bible presents the powers of darkness as a kingdom of organised evil. Satan is the director with a worldwide organisation of evil spiritual forces behind him. As we've said, he can't be everywhere at the same time, but his delegates certainly get about a bit!

Ephesians 6:10–12

'Finally, be strong in the Lord and in his mighty power. Put on the full armour of God so that you can take your stand against the devil's schemes. For our struggle is not against flesh and blood, but against the rulers, against the authorities, against the powers of this dark world and against the spiritual forces of evil in the heavenly realms.

1. *Satan*   Archangel alongside Michael.

2. *Rulers*   (Greek word *arche)* meaning: government, ruler, prince, beginning, first. The one who does something before others.

3. *Powers*   (Greek word *kosmokrator)* meaning: world rulers of darkness. Beings who affect the fate of humanity.

4. *Authorities* (Greek word *exousia*) meaning: magistrate, jurisdiction, right to act within a particular area. An authority probably below rulers.

Daniel 10:13 (compare ruler prince with prince here)

Different spheres, areas of authority. Countries, areas, towns, people groups, individuals.

In the Gospels, e.g. Matthew 12:28

Demons/evil spirits/unclean spirits = fallen angels of lower authority acting under Satan. These angels fell with Satan at his rebellion (Rev. 12:7–9). It is these spirits who speak through spiritualists during séances and also manipulate the Ouija board. Hence the dangers of such practices.

These rulers, authorities, principalities and powers are spiritual beings, fallen angels, who have delegated authority under Satan which operates at many levels, be it international, national, local or individual.

No wonder humanity has not been able to answer the world's problems merely through science, medicine, philosophy and skilful politics. Humanity without God is helpless. For a start, our battle is not just against unemployment, injustice, murder and war, but also against the spiritual forces behind them (Eph. 6:10–12).

When Hitler exterminated around six million Jews it was more than a sick, demented power-crazed man at work. His whole life was steeped in the occult and I believe that behind his evil work were strong evil principalities and powers.

How else can we make sense of African countries, racked by civil war, to the degree that we cannot get food supplies through to starving millions? These countries often have enough potential mineral resources and wealth to support themselves. Yet they are made powerless by their history, current struggles and the impact of colonialism and globalisation on their economy. Alongside these factors there is an almost 'supernatural' brutality demonstrated in many savage wars and massacres.

I read a report in a national paper about the Tottenham riots in October 1985 during which a policeman was murdered. One of his colleagues said that as darkness fell an atmosphere of evil, violence and murder descended. They knew that someone would be killed. Satan doesn't belong to any political party. His policy is murder, rape and destruction of anybody: black or white, rich or poor, policeman or unemployed. At the time of that riot Satan's forces were working overtime.

Satan's areas of activity

The only way to be clear of Satan's arena of influence is to be close to God and obey him in everything. Even then there will be times of temptation and testing which we must learn to handle. However, God wants everyone to be aware of the devil's schemes so we won't be fooled by him when he tries to pull a fast one on us (2 Cor. 2:11). It is impossible to predict exactly which way the enemy will attack. However, one thing we can be sure of is that he'll be true to his character. A land army will not attack by boat! A land army only has tanks, other land vehicles and feet! It can only use its available resources. A land army can only be just that – a land army! Similarly, Satan can only be who he is. His activity and schemes will be a direct reflection of his character. We are going to close this chapter with a quick survey of what the Bible says about his character and identify the sort of things he involves himself in.

Three Things Satan is Really Keen On

1. Idolatry

One of the names used of Satan in the Bible is Beelzebub (Mt. 12:24). No, this is not a new brand of washing-up liquid! The name literally means 'Lord of the flies' or 'Lord of idolatrous sacrifice'. Basically, the Bible points out that we worship the thing we most desire or that which we consider as the highest good. An idol is anything that replaces God's slot as number one in our lives, be it priorities, attitudes, relationships, hobbies or people. The Lord is a jealous God (see Deut. 4:15–31).

I remember a guy who was in our church, who was a skinhead and a Chelsea supporter. He had a dramatic conversion to Christianity and God did many miraculous things for him. Despite this, however, job commitments on a Sunday and Chelsea's away matches meant that he was continually missing church meetings. He was a member of the 'shed' (Chelsea 'Boot Boys') and ended up in football violence and trouble with the police. He came to me one day and shared his predicament. God had showed him that, although there is nothing wrong with football itself, his attitude was idolatrous. Unbelievably, Chelsea was number one in his life, not God. He could go no further until Jesus was back as number one. Sadly, he failed to put him first and is now a long way from living in God's kingdom.

At the thin end of idolatry are desires, ambitions and material goods that are out of God's control. There is nothing wrong with an ambition as long as it doesn't drain our love for God. For some, self-sufficiency, independence, money, body image and even science are gods.

At the thick end of idolatry are things like the occult and worship within false religions. Satan, by nature, is now an idolater and will encourage any of these. My advice is stay free of idols, and stay free!

2. *Rebellion, arrogance and pride*

A glance at Isaiah 14 and Ezekiel 28 will, along with other Bible passages (e.g. 1 Tim. 3:6), reveal the heart of Satan's character. Deep within him is the desire for conquest and power over God, which is what led him to rebel in the first place. His rebellion was vain and hopeless in the face of God's power, but Satan was proud and conceited enough to actually believe he could defeat God.

Unfortunately, within most of us there is a streak of rebellion and pride which can get us into trouble. This is certainly not a Christian characteristic. We don't like being told what to do and in pride think we always know best. A kind of superiority complex. Satan is eager to encourage those tendencies in us because if we live our lives this way we never truly obey God, and it is obedience to God's will that unlocks more of his blessing into our lives. Christians who are rebellious, proud and arrogant will be kept in a poverty of spiritual experience by this.

But Samuel replied: 'Does the LORD delight in burnt offerings and sacrifices as much as in obeying the voice of the LORD? To obey is better than sacrifice, and to heed is better than the fat of rams. For rebellion is like the sin of divination, and arrogance like the evil of idolatry. Because you have rejected the word of the LORD, he has rejected you as king' (1 Sam. 15:22–23).

3. Deception and lies

So much of the occult is subtle and deceptive. It always seems to be packaged as either Christian, scientific, mind power or simply a game. Scarcely will it be shown honestly and openly for what it is. I remember pulling into a motorway service station once, and while I was waiting to pay for my petrol I saw a book by a spiritualist medium. The cover was packaged with a harmless-looking motherly figure appealing to us to listen to these spirit messages. In my opinion, such books ought to be given a Government Health Warning, not placed alongside *Black Beauty*.

Satan is a powerful deceiver, be it leading humanity astray in the beginning (Gen. 3:1–13) or during the end times (Rev. 12:9). In fact he has blinded the minds of people so much that they can't even see God in order to believe in him (2 Cor. 4:4). I wasn't surprised, therefore, to read a story in the press of an ex-Satanist who had lied and fiddled by deception thousands of pounds out of well-meaning Christians so that he could buy objects which had been cursed. Supposedly if he didn't buy them they would ensure his destruction. I have great sympathy for the Christians involved, but it's a pity they didn't think of praying in authority to God and breaking the power of those objects. It would have been a lot cheaper.

The Christian will need to guard against deception in many areas. I'll list some of them:

1. *Pride* – 'I can make it without God.'

2. *Wealth* – There is nothing wrong with having cash, but it can be deceptive if we are not careful (Mt. 13:22). It can give us a false sense of security and immortality without God (see Lk. 12:16–21).

3. *False Teaching* – This is too vast a subject to cover here. Needless to say, there was this problem in the early church. (Read 1 Tim. 4:1–5 and Eph. 4:14.)

4. *Occult involvement* – Involvement in counterfeit spirituality is dangerous and deceptive. (Read Acts 8:9–25.) We'll see more of this later.

5. *Lies* – Satan is the father of lies (Jn. 8:44,45). If we persist in lying, in the end we will not just deceive others but even ourselves (1 Jn. 1:8).

6. *Hypocrisy* – If there is a large gap between what we say and believe and how we live as Christians, we are deceived. (Read Jas. 1:22–27.)

7. *Immorality/sin* – Sin by its nature is deceptive (Heb. 3:13).

I remember talking to a teenage Christian couple after I had mentioned in a talk that sexual intercourse outside marriage was wrong in God's eyes. They took to task saying, 'Surely it's okay if we are in love.' No matter how many Bible passages I quoted or examples I gave they still refused to listen. 'We still pray together,' they said. I quoted Psalm 66:18, which basically says that if we hold sin in our heart God won't even hear our prayers. They were talking to thin air and needed to say sorry to God, stop sleeping together, receive God's forgiveness and *then* pray together! Unfortunately they wouldn't listen and left the church to pursue Christianity their own way. Sadly, they both took drugs, their relationship broke up and the girl had a nervous breakdown and needed a short spell receiving psychiatric care. They had been caught by the deceitfulness of sin. I am not saying that everybody who gets into sexual immorality will end up on drugs and with psychiatric problems. What I am saying, however, is there's no doubt about it, *sin seriously damages your faith!*

In fact it can eventually deal it a deathblow.

Chapter 4

Horror-Scopes and All That

Things are beginning to fit into place. We have seen where the roots of the occult lie and exactly where God is in all this. We are now ready to summarise different aspects in more detail so we can learn to identify them on sight. I often have people coming to me and asking me whether I've heard of so and so, what it is, and whether or not it's dodgy. Maybe they had been talking about God to someone and found out that the person was into some form of obscure occult practice. I hope this chapter, which is a small 'Occult Directory', will be of help to you in these situations.

The Video Shop and TV Shows

Some of this chapter may seem a little remote to you. However, a trip to your local video/DVD library will show you where the general public are at and just what they like to watch on their evening off. In my local shop at least thirty of the films on display have an overt occult emphasis, and a careful second glance would reveal most of the things listed in the directory. Whether we watch directly-occult horror or 'comedy' shows about witches and demons on TV, they tell a story of the occult fascination our society has and spread a spiritual agenda which if taken seriously could be potentially harmful. They are all potential publicity for Satan's kingdom. If you want to avoid an evening watching occult propaganda it pays to be choosy when selecting what you watch these days.

The Directory

It's probably better not to read all of this directory through at once as it's not exactly a bundle of laughs. It's definitely not the stuff for late night reading after a heavy cheese supper and an overdose of hot chocolate! Use it as a resource to give you at least a very basic understanding of things you come across day by day.

Amulets/lucky charms

Objects that are worn superstitiously and carried as symbols of protection. A St Christopher necklace could certainly fall into this category, as could a 'lucky crystal'. Several reasons are given for their alleged power:

1. What they are made of. For example, many people wear copper to fend off arthritis.

2. What they look like. They may take on the form of an idol or occult symbol and be adorned with symbolic jewels.

3. How they are inscribed (words placed in them, etc.).

4. A spell that has been cast upon them. (Where 3 and 4 apply, the object is similar to a talisman.)

Animism/ancestor spirits

Tribal religions which in various ways worship the spirits of their ancestors. These spirits are believed to be able to appear in dreams, warn people of danger, as well as causing great harm. This may seem a long way from twenty-first century Britain; however, the rise of belief in 'mother earth', the popularity of Stonehenge and Glastonbury, has set some people on the path to animism, nature religion and paganism.

Apparitions (ghosts/phantoms)

Strange appearances of figures or persons (living or dead) for whatever reason.

Astral body

The spiritual, non-material body supposedly possessed by all humans (and in some beliefs all living things) which continues to exist (or separates) after bodily death. Also known as a soul body, etherial body, double spirit body, dream body or psychic body. According to spiritualists this is the vehicle for the spirit in its first state after death.

Astral plane

According to spiritualism this is the intermediate world into which the spirit passes at death. Some mediums claim they project themselves there at will.

Astral projection

A temporary experience of leaving one's body which is particularly dangerous. This is achieved by some through meditation techniques and by others through taking hallucinogenic drugs like LSD or so-called Magic Mushrooms. Others have also experienced astral projection during yoga exercises.

Astrology

Divination by often inaccurate presentations of the signs of the zodiac. Using the times, places and dates of birth, astrologers create a chart which is used to:

1. Predict future events.
2. Analyse people's characters.
3. Plan people's futures.

Aura

A force-field or energy field around the body which is normally invisible (according to those who believe in it). Certain occultists interpret these auras based on their colour, shape or brightness.

Automatic writing

Writing produced by an individual in a trance or while hallucinating, usually without their conscious awareness. This is often associated with séances.

Blood pact

A pact with the devil in your own blood to serve evil in exchange for power. Any pact with evil, whether spoken or written, is powerful and can lead to terrible bondage at the hands of the powers of darkness.

Chain letters

A letter sent with a request to copy it and send to others. It is intended to grow progressively as each new recipient writes to a number of friends. Prosperity and good luck are offered as a reward for co-operation, and a curse or ill-fortune threatened for failure to take part. Chain letters are sent to others, whereas letters of protection are like lucky charms for personal use. (See Curses, Charms, Spells, Amulets.)

Charms

A broad term including incantations (spells) and amulets, fetishes or talismans. The word originally meant 'a song of holy words' which had magical powers. When referred to an object, it refers to the spoken spell used to prepare the object.

Clairvoyance

Extrasensory or paranormal abilities to see images that are not ordinarily visible (such as ghosts or visions).

Control spirit (familiar spirit)

A medium's personal spirit, which encourages, enlightens and speaks through them during séances. It is in fact an evil spirit that is communicating, not the spirit of a dead person.

Coven

A witchcraft group usually consisting of 13 members.

Crystal gazing (crystal ball or scrying)

Divination or clairvoyance which uses a crystal ball as the means of spirit contact. Some people do this by looking upon water, fire, clouds or some other such object.

Curses

Charms intended to cause evil related to black magic.

Direct voice

While in a trance, a person/medium's voice is taken over by a control spirit or another evil spirit. Sometimes the accent or tone is a totally different voice to that of the medium (see Mk. 1:21–26).

Divination

A broad category which includes various means of attaining knowledge not available naturally. This knowledge is obtained by occult techniques which produce results that can be interpreted. For example, horoscopes are a form of divination in that astrological data is compiled and then interpreted.

Dowsing

A form of divination in which a forked rod of hazel wood, or similar construction, is used in an attempt to find underground water or minerals. This practice is sometimes still used by the Water Board today in its search for water.

Dream interpretation

A form of prediction; divination by dreams. Whilst many dreams reflect areas of our subconscious which have not been expressed during our waking moments, there are some modern books which put dream interpretation into a similar league as horoscope predictions. These books can be extremely deceptive and can provide a wide-open gateway into the occult.

Drugs

Spiritual and mental bondage produced by chemicals that create an altered state of consciousness. Many drugs give and create a similar experience to some forms of Eastern meditation like transcendental meditation (TM). The New Testament Greek word for sorcery is *pharmakia* or pharmacy. There is therefore an obvious biblical link between sorcery, the occult and drug abuse. Those who mess with drugs don't just risk physical addiction, but also demonic bondage.

Druids

Often on the news with regard to the summer solstice celebrations at Stonehenge. They were the priestly caste of pagan Celtic society. It is likely they led sacrifices and practised magic and occult healing. Obvious links with paganism, nature religion and pantheism (see Chapter 2).

Ectoplasm

Much humour was made of this in the film *Ghostbusters*, which also showed examples of direct voice and other forms of demonic manifestation. Occultists in reality claim this is a mysterious fluid-like or semi-physical substance which comes out from a medium's body.

Evil eye

The power which some are supposed to have by birth, or black magic, to cause misfortune to others.

Evocation

The calling forth of a dangerous evil spirit by the means of spoken or written word. The evoked spirit must stay at all times outside the protective pentangle, and often a special place for it is ritually marked out. An extremely dangerous process.

Extrasensory perception (ESP)

Formerly known as the 'sixth sense'. It is an experience of, a response to, or a knowledge of an event or object that could not have been gained through our normal senses. It relates to divination, clairvoyance and telepathy.

Fairies and goblins

Not here referring to children's stories. Many people who have been into LSD or Magic Mushrooms report conversations with such beings while in an altered state of consciousness. In this situation you have a medium-like experience where the person is communicating with evil spirits. The cult Emin promotes belief in fairies.

Fetish

As per amulet or charm except for the fact that a fetish is believed to be the residing place of a familiar spirit (a spirit that has developed a relationship with a person – see Direct voice).

Fire walking

A spiritualistic ceremony to show the human ability (under the influence of spiritual forces) to walk over a bed of very hot coals without physical harm. This is often faked, but by no means always.

Fortune telling

Foretelling of the future. Predictive divination.

Freemasonry

A secret society based on symbolic occult-type activity. Many people think that Freemasonry is non-religious, and it does appear at first glance to be pseudo-Christian, but in reality there are many reasons why a Christian would find it impossible to be a Freemason too.[3]

Geomancy (fortune bones/dice)

Divination by interpreting the patterns made by objects that have been thrown on the ground. Patterns are sometimes interpreted by certain rules, but more often by intuitive recognition (i.e. they make it up as they go along!).

---

[3] For further reading: Ankerberg and Weldon, *Facts on the Masonic Lodge*, Harvest House, 2002.

Ghosts

An apparition of an earthbound nature spirit, or a departed soul depending on the occultist's world-view. In reality, I believe that a ghost is either a mirage or a visible manifestation of an evil spirit designed to deceive people into further occult experimentation or practice. Many films are based on ghosts and from time to time ghosts break into the media too. At the time of writing there have been a number of reports of ghostly apparitions in hospitals across our nation.

Graphology

Divination of character or health by analysing handwriting. Usually more of a superstition or a vague assumption as to a person's character rather than a spiritualistic phenomenon. However, it is used by some for telepathy.

Hallowe'en

All Hallows Eve. The 31 October witch festival. One of the four sabbats of coven witchcraft taken from the four great festivals of the ancient pagan Celts. It is believed by many occultists that Satan walks the earth on these sabbats.

Hex

An evil spell.

Horoscope

See Astrology. A diagram of the relative positions of planets and signs of the zodiac at a specific time (e.g. birth). It's used in foretelling events in a person's life. The fact is, constellations shift; consequently, astrologers today don't see the planets in the same position as the astrologer of 4–5,000 years ago did. Also, new planets have been discovered: Uranus in 1781, Neptune in 1846 and Pluto in 1930 – and yet there has been absolutely no change in the astrological system!

Astrology is a superstition which has often been called 'the foolish daughter of a wise mother – astronomy'[4] (the study of the stars).

Invocation

The calling forth of a so-called 'good spirit' by words, whether written or spoken.

Kabbalah, Qabbalah or Cabala

Jewish occult mysticism. It covers various forms of fortune-telling, magic, altered states of consciousness and spiritualism integrated into a complex philosophical system. Pop star and actress Madonna is reported to be a devotee of the Kabbalah.

Kirlian photography

A high frequency electrical process which produces a photo-like image of an apparent electrical field that allegedly surrounds living beings. It is considered to be a means of photographing the aura and diagnosing illness and depression.

Levitation

The lifting of a person or object from the ground by totally non-physical, material means. It is achieved through the exertion of psychic powers.

Ley lines

Straight geological lines of spiritual force which some adherents of pagan religions believe were discovered

---

[4] Source unknown.

and used in the Neolithic period. Their existence is said to be demonstrated by the many alignments between religious sites. There is no archaeological support for this view, though many ancient religious sites do seem to be aligned with one another. Glastonbury and Stonehenge are key sites where ley lines are said to converge.

Lifting game

Three or four people are able to lift the weight of a full-grown adult with just their fingertips. A magic formula is chanted after which the person is lifted. This could be a mixture of levitation, self-hypnosis and occult magic.

Magic (black and white)

Exercising power or attempting to manipulate evil spirits. The idea is to subvert or manipulate or dominate people or situations for your own ends by spirit power. *Black* magic is supposed to be for selfish or destructive purposes. *White* magic is for 'benevolent' purposes. In reality both black and white magic are evil and dangerous, and lie at the centre of the occult.

Medium (psychic)

A person who is sensitive or open to be used by occult powers to the extent that they convey information from these powers to others. In spiritualism, the communication is supposed to be from dead people, via the medium, to living people. A mental medium will transmit only messages, while a physical medium will attempt to use meditation and other forms of physical manifestation.

Necromancy

Divination by consulting the dead: often used of spiritualism or conducting séances.

Numerology

Divination based on the symbolic interpretation of the numbers one to nine. People's names, birth dates and other significant events are reduced to digits and interpreted.

Omens

Divination by means of interpreting unusual or uncontrollable events, for example the flight of birds. It's a form of fortune telling.

Ouija board

A means of communicating with evil spirits and also of demonstrating ESP. A board with the alphabet and the words *Yes* and *No* on it is placed on a table. A glass is turned upside down and each participant rests a finger on it and asks a spirit to move the glass. Many people have been plagued with fear, depression, rage, anger, insanity and have even attempted to commit suicide after involvement with Ouija. It is to be avoided at all costs.

Palmistry

Divination. The assessment of personality and foretelling the future by examining hands.

Paranormal

As related to psychic research. Phenomena that are beyond normality and supernatural.

Parapsychology

A field of study related to investigating telepathy and clairvoyance.

Pendulum

An instrument that can be used in the place of a divining rod in dowsing. The swinging of a small object on the end of a chain or cord. Pendulums are sometimes swung over people in supernatural healing and other forms of divination.

Phrenology

Divination by examining the contours of the skull.

Poltergeists

Noisy ghosts. A haunting phenomenon producing violent noises and physical manifestations like writing on a wall and the levitation of furniture. Poltergeists tend to be focused around an individual (perhaps a familiar spirit). A person that I prayed for once had this type of activity occurring in her house. After prayer it seemed that the activity ceased.

Possession

Usually used to describe a person that is subject to an extreme form of demonic infiltration, due usually to occult involvement. The Bible doesn't talk of possession as ownership, but as demonisation or having an evil spirit. Both Jesus Christ and the early church on his behalf demonstrated that God has the power to set people free from this kind of oppression (Mt. 8:28–34; Acts 8:4–8).

Premonitions

Advance warnings about specific events or situations. Sometimes this is clairvoyance or ESP.

Role-playing games

Games or books within which the participant is encouraged to adopt another personality through imagination and fantasy. Many games and books of this type contain frequent references to black magic, clairvoyance and evil spirits. There are some good fantasy books about such as those by C. S. Lewis or Tolkien, but generally care should be taken here.

Rune

See *Spell*.

Sabbat

A midnight assembly of witches and sorcerers to renew allegiance to the devil through various rites, often involving animal sacrifice and sexual perversion.

Satanism

Worship and service to the devil (Satan). It is often a ritualistic form of worship which is sometimes based on a twisted, upside-down rip-off of medieval Roman Catholicism. Satanists delight in turning things morally and physically the wrong way round, hence they use the Lord's Prayer backwards.

Spell

An incantation, chant or spiritual formula used to influence another person either 'positively' or 'negatively' (then seen as a curse).

Tarot

Divination by card laying, either with tarot cards or other types of standard playing cards.

Telepathy

Mind reading. The ability to transfer your thoughts to another person's mind without physical means.

Trance

An altered state of consciousness induced by occult activity. A trance is generally self-induced (except in hypnotism) and is a state in which a person is particularly open to demonic attack.

Trick or treat

Part of the celebration of Hallowe'en. Originally in the USA, in the nineteenth century, boys and young men went on orgies of vandalism. The custom developed with children knocking on doors and asking for sweets and cakes as an inducement for them not to inflict damage (a trick or treat). Today the tricks are somewhat milder. This tradition has its roots in the past and the occult influence of Hallowe'en. Some of the tricks have even been likened to curses.

Unidentified Flying Objects (UFOs)

A phenomenon where flying saucers and spacecrafts are seen and alien beings are contacted. This is sometimes an occult experience and many people who have taken LSD, Magic Mushrooms, or had an experience of an altered state of consciousness, have had hallucinations of UFOs.

Voodoo

An African-originated Haitian form of magic and divination using effigies (models of people which can be cursed). This produces altered states of consciousness and induces demonic influence.

Warlock

A male practitioner of black magic, a sorcerer or male witch.

Wicca

Nature religion just like witchcraft. It is not as old as claimed, but was founded by Gerald Gardner in the twentieth century.

Witchcraft, witches

A vague description of the practice of magic, or divination, by people who may or may not practise Satanism.

Wizard

Sometimes a male witch, it means 'wise one' and may describe any male occultist.

The directory may seem a little weird upon first reading. But wait a minute, have you read a Harry Potter book or seen the movies? A number of the scenarios outlined in the directory happen in the films. The author has clearly researched the occult!

I actually think there is a lot of good in the Harry Potter books. Creativity, adventure and a good moral behind the story. However, I do find both the focus on and accuracy of the description of occult activity a little too precise for my liking. As parents, my wife and I didn't discourage our kids from reading the books, but we did take time to talk and if necessary pray through the context with them. Having a 'hero' who is involved in the occult is not a good thing, but having a 'hero' who is brave, honest and loving is not too bad!

A Real-Life Example

Here we have observed only the edges of the occult, but we can see that it is both far-reaching and particularly dangerous. For some of you, the names and experiences will be familiar, as past involvement has already taken its toll on your life. For others, it will still seem a little unreal.

'Can this be true?' you may ask. 'Can it really be that dangerous?' Well, I've asked a friend of mine to tell his story. It's the tale of a teenager with a lot of curiosity and street cred who, through a series of dire coincidences and his own rebellion, became hopelessly ensnared by Satan's forces. That is, until Jesus Christ set him free.

At the age of eleven, I was very much the normal school kid, looking forward to going to secondary school and all its involvements. Yet very soon all this normality was going to change.

My life was shattered when halfway through the first year of school I was sexually assaulted on numerous occasions by my scout leader. I remember hearing my religious education teacher talking about men approaching children, and after the lesson I went up and told him what was happening. Instantly my world changed. I missed school for a few days and was interviewed by policemen. Tension around the home grew. Oddly, though, I did not feel a part of it any more. I began to detach myself from the situation and through all this upheaval I remained impartial and totally emotionless.

As the school year progressed, I began to rebel, fighting, arguing and dominating situations. My best friend was put into another class and we drifted apart. That particular school year ended for me on the other side of the law, being cautioned for setting fire to a telephone box. When my mother came to punish me for 'causing so much trouble' I once again shrunk away from the situation, finding my own world through which to observe the 'goings on'.

That summer, we went camping in the Lake District. That world offered me a sanctuary – the countryside of mountains, lakes and rivers, coupled with the vast expanse of solitude (me alone with nature). I made friends with the earth, the beauty and mystery of my surroundings, and it allowed my imagination to blend with reality. When we left, I sat in the back of the car, staring out of the back window and wishing I could have been left there.

School started again, but this time my mind was elsewhere. I had blocked out the memories of the earlier year, yet this school was not the same. The same faces, same teachers, but I did not gel there any longer. My interest was beginning to look elsewhere, for something I could understand and be in control of. When Christmas arrived, I looked forward to a return to family and normality, yet my expectations were never reached, and throughout the events I watched as though through a camera lens. Then, to my surprise, all seemed to return to normal. I worked at school, began to play rugby and began to enjoy myself, having fun, making friends, having sly fags with the other school kids, sneaking off to the chippy at dinner break and other such things.

Then, I remember going to the bus stop one morning and meeting a friend who told me that my best friend at primary school had died. At first I did not believe him, but when it was announced officially at school I was so rocked I left soon after assembly and dawdled my way home along the canal, thinking all about the mischief we used to get up to. His death was the event that sent me straight back to my old self.

Later that same month, I received an invitation from my deceased friend's mother to go around for tea. I went to see the lady and was so enthralled by her that I began to visit her regularly. I enjoyed seeing her as she always had cakes, tea and biscuits for me. Soon a deep friendship formed; she offered me a sanctuary from normality. We exchanged comfort through sharing our grief. I loaned her books that I had read, and we would sit up for nights talking about anything. We would go for driving expeditions into the countryside and soon she found a permanent place in my life. It was a permanence that I could not break.

It was at this time that I began to smoke dope. I found it wonderful to be able to relax and drift away, smiling and laughing. All through that summer I smoked whenever it was available. I would miss days from school in order to get stoned. I would sneak away from home and smoke with my friend's mother. The more I smoked, the more vague my situation became and I liked that. She would talk about meditation and encounters with other consciousnesses. She showed me how to meditate properly and instructed me how to use meditation. I took to this instantly as it heightened my awareness when I was stoned and gave me instant access to another plane of existence. Astral projection and transcendental meditation came next – trying to project our minds towards another being, communing with other spirit levels, and attempting to talk to each other through our minds, inviting any friendly spirits to direct our paths.

All this led to a deeper desire to avoid the real world and become the escapist. School life by this time was almost non-existent. My home life was unbearable. I disliked my mother, always arguing and often fighting. The more I smoked dope, the greater the interest in meditation, and the more magic I involved myself with the more distant I became.

By the time I was fifteen I had been caught for shop-lifting. I was always stealing money for dope and was well into meditation (when stoned). But now Ouija boards, séances, runic magic, tarot cards, paganism (the worship of nature) had captivated my imagination.

I was depressed, only escaping when stoned. That year I had my first encounter with Christianity. I committed my life to Jesus and started to attend a local church. But the continuation of my occult involvement and the confusion surrounding my life saw to it that I was not prayed for.

I soon drifted back to my old ways and I left the church. I now had a fanatical interest in acid, opium and Magic Mushrooms. I would take acid whenever I could get it, eat Mushrooms in the autumn and smoke opiated dope whenever I could. My awareness of the occult grew, but in a different vein. I worshipped the night, the moon, the stars and the forces of the earth. Sometimes I would 'trip' with my friend's mother. Often dread presences would manifest themselves, and I opened up in order to avoid a bad trip. This whole process soon led to an interest in African magic and Caribbean voodooism.

Finally, I was kicked out of school and soon after that I was arrested for burglary. My life was crumbling, and I continued to avoid God. The drug taking went on for another year. My occult involvement became deeper. That same year, my parents were divorced and I left home. Still I smoked and 'tripped' and practised magic, unable to stop what I now recognised as a downward spiral.

Then I started seeing an Eastern mystic's daughter. That relationship started well and I moved to London. It was there that I gave up drugs, but started to drink very heavily. Still I craved spiritual enlightenment, talking with the mystic about Hindu meditation, yoga, Kundalini meditation and the philosophies of Carl Jung. She encouraged me, saying I had the potential to make a great teacher if I would train for it. My relationship with my girlfriend plummeted after she had an abortion.

Rapidly my world was dying. Then I began to write to God in my diary. The more I wrote to him, the worse my mental state became. Soon I became suicidal. But I still wrote to God, hating him for my life, yet knowing he was the only person left for me. I had no money, no home, no girlfriend, and no relationship with my family – just Jesus.

In December 1986, at the age of nineteen, I finally couldn't take the madness any more. In a confused state, I caught a train to Chichester to talk with my old church leader. When I arrived, we sat and talked. He offered to pray for me. I asked for forgiveness from Jesus and knew that the mistakes of the past were forgiven. I felt free for the first time since the abuse.

The power of God released me from the guilt of my past actions. I can now with hand on heart say I have encountered the living God and found a fresh purpose and meaning in life.

Chapter 5

The New Age – Is it Really New?

So far we have looked at many different strains of the occult. Satan tends to call the same old tune. And so we've seen that many of his more current schemes – for example, newspaper horoscopes – bear a direct relation to the astrology which has been practised for thousands of years and condemned by the Bible as far back as the time of Moses. As we take a look at the emergence of the New Age Movement in this chapter, we need to observe that the vast majority of its views and practices are not new. They find their roots in the Eastern world-views we looked at in Chapter 2.

Every so often in the pop charts an artist or band will release a 'cover version'. This is a rework of an old hit. The hit *Spirit in the Sky* by Gareth Gates is a good example, being a rework of an old number by Norman Greenbaum, revamped later by Doctor and the Medics. Songs like *Eternal Flame* by Atomic Kitten, and *Mandy* by Westlife were cover versions. The one thing that all these have in common is that no matter how much they speed up or slow down the song, and no matter how different the arrangements, the tune remains the same. The stamp of the original writer is still there.

The New Age Movement is like this. It is a rework and remix of Hinduism, Buddhism and Taoism which has been adapted and commercialised to appeal to the Western market. Nevertheless, it cannot shake off its roots.

What is the New Age?

Pick up a magazine or a newspaper and it won't be long before you come across it. Articles on 'New Age', Developing Your Human Potential', 'The Power of Positive Thinking', 'Alternative Medicine', 'Eastern Meditation' and 'Yoga' abound. How does it all link up? Well, let me first make it clear that the New Age Movement is not a single definitive organisation but is an umbrella term covering a wide range of influences and different emerging movements. These movements can be religious, pseudo-religious, pseudoscientific, supposedly non-religious and even allegedly medical! One thing most of them have in common is their Eastern world-view which is directly incompatible with Christianity, being linked chiefly with Hinduism, Buddhism or Taoism.

The danger is that the movement is generally so subtle that even many Christians have been drawn into it without realising. Once in the fold, the chips are down. The Christian idea of God and spirituality becomes more and more blurred until you find yourself far away from the clear teaching of the Bible, and our chances of maintaining or finding a real friendship with God through Jesus Christ are being gradually undermined.

Where has this come from?

Much of the New Age thinking has emerged from the counter-cultural movements of the 1960s. The hippie movement with its characteristic permissive 'new morality' (neither new nor moral) was also heavily influenced by Eastern mysticism, drugs and the occult. The Beatles led the way by linking with the Maharishi Mahesh Yogi and his transcendental meditation (TM). The Age of Aquarius had dawned, and people in vast numbers ran headlong into various forms of Buddhism, Hinduism and the like. This movement became attractive to many humanists who, although not believing in God, were working in vain towards an age when humanity would evolve to the place of paradise on earth. The Age of Aquarius with its positive assertions offered fresh hope and attracted many of them. Also many agnostics and even atheists were drawn to the movement through its pseudo-scientific approach.

TM particularly saw rapid growth due to its deceptive and false claim to be scientific and not a religion. This seems a sick joke to the informed Christian observer, but nevertheless, many well meaning people were duped into subscribing, and often handed over the whole of their worldly wealth to the Maharishi Mahesh Yogi, or some other guru.

The Aquarians of the 1960s have moved on in large strides. They've cut their hair and shed the hippie image. In fact, it has been said that the generation that reacted so violently against the materialism of the 1960s has become the most materialistic generation America has ever known. Although the long hair, kaftans and simple lifestyles have largely disappeared, one thing has remained: the Eastern philosophy and religion. The 1960s Aquarians have grown up and infiltrated business, religion, art, science, music, medicine, health, education, psychology, politics and entertainment with their spirituality and world-view.

Here we have the New Age Movement (NAM) in comparison with the Age of Aquarius. It is subtler, more sophisticated, more acceptable and more mature. It has both grown and grown up, along with its followers. In the 1960s yoga, Eastern meditation, psychic powers, holistic medicine, and the like, would have mainly seemed weird, occult and only for the fringe few. Today, they are respectable, acceptable norms to many. New Age propaganda has been extremely effective.

New Age Traits

Among 'New Agers' a belief in reincarnation proliferates, with yoga and meditation being a part of normal life. Astrology, spiritualism and many more 'orthodox' forms of the occult also abound. Because of the mix of Eastern beliefs, a confusion of religion has emerged. Many traditional Hindus would in fact be incensed to see how the New Age Movement has adjusted and adapted its philosophy at will to suit the Western consumer. Within this mishmash, the general theory would be that *all religions lead to the same God.*

The George Harrison song *My Sweet Lord* which mixes the Jewish/Christian proclamation of worship 'Hallelujah' with 'Hare Krishna' the Tantric chant that Hare Krishna followers use to invoke the spirit deity Krishna. By definition, the two exclamations are totally different. 'Hallelujah' literally means 'Praise the Lord'. It is a personal cry of worship to the living, personal God of creation. 'Hare Krishna', on the other hand, is a chant to Krishna, not the Almighty God of the Christian. It is a chant designed to invoke a spirit reaction and advance realisation. *The Matrix* series of films follows the same pattern merging all sorts of Hindu and Buddhist thinking with Christian symbolism to provide a film which can be interpreted in many different ways. Depending on how you look at it, at times it appears to be an allegory of Christian things, at others it seems to be totally New Age.

Basically, it is in some cases totally dishonest, and in other cases misconceived, to assert that all religions lead to the same God. As we've seen by the Christian definition, Hindus and Buddhists don't even believe in God, and the requirements for salvation are totally different. Still, it suits the twenty-first-century consumer: no moral absolutes to tie you down, and you can sample whatever mix of religion you feel like, at whatever level you feel like because it all leads to God. This is a deception many have fallen for, and Christians would want to warn that far from all religions leading to the same God, some lead straight into the occult.

Watch out for false prophets. They come to you in sheep's clothing, but inwardly they are ferocious wolves. By their fruit you will recognise them. Do people pick grapes from thornbushes, or figs from thistles? Likewise every good tree bears good fruit, but a bad tree bears bad fruit. A good tree cannot bear bad fruit, and a bad tree cannot bear good fruit. Every tree that does not bear good fruit is cut down and thrown into the fire. Thus, by their fruit you will recognise them.

Not everyone who says to me, 'Lord, Lord,' will enter the kingdom of heaven, but only he who does the will of my Father who is in heaven. Many will say to me on that day, 'Lord, Lord, did we not prophesy in your name, and in your name drive out demons and perform many miracles?' Then I will tell them plainly, 'I never knew you. Away from me, you evildoers!' (Mt. 7:15–23).

Jesus answered: 'Watch out that no-one deceives you. For many will come in my name, claiming, "I am the Christ," and will deceive many. You will hear of wars and rumours of wars, but see to it that you are not alarmed. Such things must happen, but the end is still to come. Nation will rise against nation, and kingdom against kingdom. There will be famines and earthquakes in various places. All these are the beginning of birth-pains.

'Then you will be handed over to be persecuted and put to death, and you will be hated by all nations because of me. At that time many will turn away from the faith and will betray and hate each other, and many false prophets will appear and deceive many people. Because of the increase of wickedness, the love of most will grow cold, but he who stands firm to the end will be saved. And this gospel of the kingdom will be preached in the whole world as a testimony to all nations, and then the end will come' (Mt. 24:4–14).

At that time if anyone says to you, 'Look, here is the Christ!' or, 'There he is!' do not believe it. For false Christs and false prophets will appear and perform great signs and miracles to deceive even the elect – if that were possible. See, I have told you ahead of time.

So if anyone tells you, 'There he is, out in the desert,' do not go out; or, 'Here he is, in the inner rooms,' do not believe it. For as the lightning comes from the east and flashes to the west, so will be the coming of the Son of Man' (Mt. 24:23–27).

Reincarnation

Reincarnation is the theory that when a body dies, the soul transmigrates – it is reborn into another body. Because of this, everybody will have experienced previous lives, and death will herald the entrance into yet another life by means of reincarnation. This never-ending process of death and rebirth is called the Wheel of Samsara. New Agers have taken this ancient belief and packaged it for the modern consumer. Today, it has become that sense of *déjà vu* which says: 'I've been to this place at some time before; maybe in my previous life I was a famous king, politician, or public figure.' Many leading New Agers have claimed just that. It is seen very much as a kind of 'upward evolution' whereby humanity is gradually being upgraded, both on an individual level and as a race of people.

This is totally at odds with the classic and original understandings of reincarnation. Far from being an upward step it is seen as a judgement. In fact the whole purpose of yoga and meditation is to reach realisation, godhood or *nirvana*, and by doing so escape its awful continued clutches.

Running alongside this is the principle of karma which numerous pop songs talk about. The word 'karma' literally means 'destiny' (i.e. your predestination). Karma is the law or principle of retribution whereby all an individual's deeds in his past lives are added up and together determine the quality of his next life. If you are a bad person, your next karma could mean a relegation down the social ladder, or what is known as the caste system. You may be born handicapped in some way, or even become an animal! If you're good, you will be one step nearer to *nirvana*; a promotion up the ladder will be in order next time round. However, the fear of judgement rules, and there are no guarantees. Slip-ups could seriously damage your karma.

These beliefs, however, don't just affect us personally. They can also dictate how we treat our neighbours. For instance, within the Hindu mindset it is seen as futile to help the poor or disabled and care for the suffering. If a person is suffering, it is as a result of evil carried out during previous lives and they must not be lifted away from the punishment as they will only receive it again in their next karma. As a result, some enterprises launched in India to relieve suffering have been opposed by the Hindus. The law of karma apparently should not be tampered with.

Of course, these beliefs are totally at odds with biblical Christianity. Scripture declares that 'man is destined to die once, and after that to face judgment' (Heb. 9:27). Not even a hint of reincarnation there. When Jesus was dying on the cross he didn't say to the dying man alongside him, 'Well, here's to the next karma,' but talked of heaven saying, 'I tell you the truth, today you will be with me in paradise' (Lk. 23:43). Christians know there is no such thing as the continual yoke of reincarnation. Not only can we experience the ongoing forgiveness of sins (1 Jn. 1:9), but as a result have no need to fear judgement, particularly the judgement of God. 'Therefore, there is now no condemnation [judgement] for those who are in Christ Jesus' (Rom. 8:1).

Rather than the monotonous despair of reincarnation, Christianity offers the reality of eternity with Jesus Christ. Paul was so excited about this that he looked forward to being with Jesus after his death, saying: 'I am torn between the two: I desire to depart and be with Christ, which is better by far; but it is more necessary for you that I remain in the body' (Phil. 1:23, 24).

The gruesome twosome: yoga and meditation

Some things just seem to go together. Tea and milk, Tom and Jerry, trees and birds, to name but a few. Wherever one of the pair is sighted, you can be certain that the other will not be too far away. So it is with the New Age Movement, reincarnation, yoga and meditation. Yoga and meditation (it needs to be said that yoga is often a form of meditation) are two of the key practices that emerge from the beliefs I have outlined so far. How then are we to relate to them?

Well, I believe that it is not enough to make statements like: 'They have helped many different people'; 'My yoga teacher is such a pleasant person'; 'It's helped me overcome tension'; or, 'If it works it must be right.' As we've seen so far, not everything that glitters is gold. Satan is a deceiver and not all his schemes and ploys seem bad at first glance. I would certainly not want to say that they don't work, but I *would* want to question their origins. A person may receive a blood transfusion after an accident which initially accelerates his recovery significantly. However, if the blood's origin is not checked and declared free from all foreign bodies and disease, the patient may end up with a worse problem than he had in the first place. The sense of relief as the transfusion received may turn to horror as the real truth of the situation emerges. So it is, I believe, with many of these techniques.

Yoga.   Yoga is firmly rooted in Hinduism (and Buddhism) and in its original form is not seen as an exercise, but as a form of worship. Every position adopted is a form of meditation and worship designed to invoke a spirit reaction. The Hindu god Shiva is the Lord of yoga. One yoga practitioner I talked to, who would not describe herself as a Hindu but a New Ager, said, 'When in yoga you communicate with Shiva, surely that's the same as worshipping the God of the Christian.' No matter how much I explained the difference between Eastern and Christian concepts of God and Reality, she refused to listen. It remains that Shiva is the god of yoga, not mighty God. Much yoga is conducted at the foot of an idol and its aim is to assist emptiness and join the person to Brahman or absolute nothingness. The actual word 'yoga' means 'to be yoked with Brahman'. It is impossible to reconcile this in any way with biblical Christianity.

Yoga forms include: *prana* (meaning soul) or breathing exercises, *leah* or dissolving the mind, *sidhis* (meaning intellect or psyche) which involves the use of psychic power and levitation, *asama* or the use of physical positions, *raja yoga* or yoga of the mind, and *Tantric yoga* which resembles black magic involving sorcery and the invoking of evil spirits.

The most common form of yoga at present is *hatha yoga* which involves the use of different positions as a means of meditation. Often a chant (mantra) will be used. This is a sacred word or syllable used to enhance concentration. The mantra can mean a chant or the casting of a spell, and when used it will be recited continually in a robotic manner to assist the neutralisation of the mind, will and emotions that is necessary for realisation. The word or syllable involved is often the name of a Hindu god or a part of the Hindu Vedic literature (psalms of praise), though any potential meditators are told that the mantra is meaningless and only a means to an end.

It is interesting that only in the West is yoga marketed purely as an exercise. In Hinduism there is no way that yoga can be separated from its religious roots, though many New Age teachers try to say that is either not religious, compatible with Christianity ('Why, *I'm* a Christian!'), or that it is purely exercise. In my opinion they are either genuinely misguided or embarking on a great con to draw more and more people into their fold. There is much talk of releasing of vital energy in the body through the exercises. Hindus call this energy the *kundalini* or snake force. In the Bible the snake is often used to describe Satan (Gen. 3:2, Rev. 20:2), whereas in Hinduism the snake is worshipped (along with most other 'things'). For instance, Shiva the destroyer is always pictured with many snakes hanging all over him.

I find the presence of the 'snake force' in yoga particularly disturbing, and it leads me to ask, 'Who or what is the power behind yoga?' It is interesting to note that the positions adopted all have particular purposes not related to exercise or muscle improvement. The cobra position, for instance, is reputed to help the release and development of psychic powers. Can yoga then be divorced from all spiritual connotations and used purely as a physical relaxation exercise? Personally, I don't believe it can. Maybe it is possible that someone may have limited involvement without too much harm being done. However, those who progress in yoga will inevitably be drawn into the occult, Eastern mysticism and maybe even into transcendental meditation – described by the Maharishi himself as 'a path of self-hypnotism'.

If you believe that yoga and meditation (as well as some of the other practices we will see in the next chapter) work, what is the basis on which they work? Unfortunately, many people get involved without clear thinking; without asking, 'What is the power behind this?' If it is believed they work because of the underlying philosophy, then it is clearly a religious practice. If it is believed they work from a purely scientific point of view, I believe people will nevertheless still find themselves adopting patterns of behaviour that have no rationale except in the underlying philosophy. Either way, the philosophy will affect the participant. Therefore, these practices cannot be neutral, and neither can they be divorced from their religious roots.

Meditation. 'What's wrong with meditation? After all it's in the Bible.' This is a question I'm often asked. My answer is almost always that it depends what is meant by 'meditation'. We are back to the confusion of terms covered in Chapter 2. The New Age concept of meditation is a totally different kettle of fish to the meditation talked of in the Bible. The Eastern meditator may use yoga and mantras in the process and will be looking for a totally different effect. Meditation will be an effort to empty the mind, and to be rid of all emotion and rationality in an attempt to be 'absorbed into the one'. The Christian product is entirely different. It will involve, not an emptying of the mind, but a filling of it with, for example, an aspect of God's character or a particular portion of the Bible. Christian meditation is not an emptying, vacuum experience but one of being filled with God's goodness and truth. It is a concentration of tangible facts, not an escape from normal consciousness. Perhaps what we need is Christians to develop a means of exercise and meditation which does not deny spirituality, but connects people more wholesomely with Jesus Christ.

The problem with the Eastern form of meditation is the vacuum it creates. Sometimes a person will find himself in a trance-like, almost hypnotic, state during which all his normal senses of will, morality, reasoning and feeling become anaesthetised. It is at this point of total passivity that a person is particularly vulnerable to manipulation and domination by others, or infiltration by occult powers.

The Bible paints the picture of a God who can be with us in all places and circumstances by the power of his Holy Spirit. Within that truth there is a definite place for stillness, quiet, and a drawing to one side for prayer, praise and Bible study. In Psalm 46 God exhorts the people to 'Be still, and know that I am God' (v. 10a). In a society full of stress, movement and activity, it becomes increasingly important to stay close to God and be filled with his peace.

However, Christian stillness is not an empty vacuum; it is coming to the place where we realise God's greatness, his power and strength, and that he is our Protector and Saviour. As a result, all our anxieties, hyperactivity, insecurities and fears are stilled and dealt with. We are left with an imprint, not of the cares of the world, but with the presence of God himself which is not emptiness but 'love, joy, peace, patience, kindness, goodness, faithfulness, gentleness and self-control' (Gal. 5:22).

Christian peace is not a trance-like state of emptiness, an escape from rationality and the real world to realisation. Neither is it a state of mind arrived at by some form of exercise or a relaxation technique. It is being at peace with God through the death and resurrection of Jesus Christ. We are able to receive God's forgiveness, healing and the gift of eternal life right now. This transforms every area of our lives and affects the whole of our being so that no area remains untouched by the blessing, assurance and Lordship of Jesus. This, in short, is real peace.

> Come to me, all you who are weary and burdened, and I will give you rest. Take my yoke upon you and learn from me, for I am gentle and humble in heart, and you will find rest for your souls (Mt. 11:28,29).

> Rejoice in the Lord always. I will say it again: Rejoice! Let your gentleness be evident to all. The Lord is near. Do not be anxious about anything, but in everything, by prayer and petition, with thanksgiving, present your requests to God. And the peace of God, which transcends all understanding, will guard your hearts and your minds in Christ Jesus (Phil. 4:4–7).

Chapter 6

From Veggie Burgers to Karate Chops – The New Age Movement in Action

If we can imagine the New Age Movement as a cruise liner, perhaps in the last chapter we were having a guided tour of the engine room, bridge and the ship's navigation equipment. We looked at the movements, roots, main characteristics and major beliefs that reveal the port of origin and the destination of the vessel. In this chapter, we are going to sample just some of the vast amount of amusements, facilities and recreational activities that are offered on board. It is these activities that dominate the attention of the passenger for 99 per cent of the time. How many people on the QE2 ask for a tour of the engine rooms when there are other more instantly appealing activities on offer? Thousands of people travel on her every year, but how many get to the heart of the ship's structure and see what really drives her?

So it is with the New Age Movement. She has many passengers that take her merely at face value. Their interest lies in consuming as much of her plentiful bounty as possible. Very few people check the safety measures, how seaworthy she is, or whether indeed the correct course has been set. Some of the practices we examine in this chapter will be household names; others will not be so well known. My plea is not for a mindless paranoid fear of these practices, nor for a bigoted 'crusade' in opposition; it is for a balanced, clear evaluation of them. What is of God and in harmony with the Bible can be gratefully embraced. What is at odds with these criteria must be firmly rejected.

Areas of Operation

The range of New Age operation is vast, covering many different spheres of life and lifestyles. As a result, I only have room for a brief coverage here, but hope that enough will be said to help you to develop your own opinions. Perhaps it would not be an overstatement to say that everybody, in the course of general living, will at one time or another be confronted directly by an aspect of the New Age Movement. As people with an Eastern world-view live and move in society, naturally their perspectives are having a lasting effect, particularly in the realms of business, medicine, general health and lifestyle.

Business

We live in a competitive, high-flying, consumer-based society. Never in the history of humanity has there been so much change at every level, to such an extent that sociologists have diagnosed us as suffering from 'future shock'. Coupled with this is the ever-present pressure to win, succeed, keep up with the Joneses, and maintain a steady climb up the social ladder. A person's worth is very much measured against his ability to deliver the goods and to stay on top. The order of the day is 'dog eat dog' as we maintain a performance mentality, keeping one step ahead of our nearest rivals.

Such intense pressure creates a career merry-go-round. The momentum of work and the pressure to succeed makes it impossible to disembark, yet the continual movement creates a dizziness that will eventually affect the victim's physical and emotional wellbeing adversely. Due to this, stress-related diseases are on the increase. For instance, stomach ulcers and heart disease are prevalent, while other people find themselves turning to alcohol or tranquillisers to release pressure or to give them 'Dutch courage'. Family life becomes threatened, and as a result the divorce rate continues to increase.

Where can the frustrated businessperson turn to for help in the midst of this stress-filled existence? Well, conventional medicine has been able to help some, others have perhaps found help in Christianity, while still others have had to significantly cut down on their activity and take more exercise. This understandably has worried many employers. After all, stress creates illness, which ultimately cuts productivity, which in turn reduces profits! This emotional, physical and spiritual vacuum must be filled.

Enter the New Age Movement with its armoury of treatments and relaxation techniques. Have hypnosis or acupuncture to cure that habit. Develop your full human potential, expand your mind, realise the power of positive thinking, explore your psychic capabilities, and all this will give you a greater capacity for more success. The force or power is in you, have faith in yourself, it just needs to be released. Use visualisation to imagine into being the things you want. The hollow vacuum created by yoga meditation seems particularly attractive in the face of all the intense activity we have observed. Many cults like Scientology (also TM) have gained access to the business world through this route as the spiritual gulf created by the excesses of materialism become more and more pronounced. Some large companies have commissioned courses that advocate many New Age techniques, while others have installed a meditation room in their home base to encourage relaxation.

I have great sympathy for anyone who gets enmeshed in the machinery of the business merry-go-round, and believe that those people deserve help in their battle to conquer all the related problems. Obviously there is nothing wrong with relaxing or having a positive outlook on life. These things, among others, can be very helpful when it comes to the release of stress. However, I don't believe an involvement in Eastern mysticism is the answer. We need to be careful that what is packaged as a course in stress relief to help the person in business is not in reality an induction into the New Age Movement.

> See to it that no-one takes you captive through hollow and deceptive philosophy, which depends on human tradition and the basic principles of this world rather than on Christ (Col. 2:8).

> Come to me, all you who are weary and burdened, and I will give you rest. Take my yoke upon you and learn from me, for I am gentle and humble in heart, and you will find rest for your souls. For my yoke is easy and my burden is light (Mt. 11:28–30).

Medicine

Unfortunately, our society is also a place where there is much illness, sickness and suffering. The inevitability of death is something that will haunt most of those who have no assurance of eternal life through a relationship with Jesus Christ. In the midst of illness we can be thankful to God for those in the medical profession and the many wonderful scientific advances they have made, enabling them either to cure the problem, prevent it or relieve the pain and symptoms. However, the value of any scientific and medical discovery or treatment must be decided on grounds other than simply, 'Does it work?' Even in this arena, we must ask, 'Is the cure ethical?' or, 'On what basis does it work?' This is not always an easy process, but it is very necessary if we are to prevent people receiving treatments that they will later regret.

We need to ask, for instance, is the experimentation on human embryos valid in order to gain information? Is abortion justifiable, or is it the murder of an unborn child? Is the use of hypnosis justified, bearing in mind that historically it is an occult practice? The person who only has results in mind will say, 'If it works, use it', while many more ethically-minded people within the medical profession would want to consider a cure or treatment carefully before allowing its use. As Christians, we can't afford simply to accept and absorb everything the world offers us. We must continue to ask questions about the origins and composition of many treatments that are on offer.

Alongside the continual ethical dilemma facing the medical profession is an underlying disillusionment expressed by some about conventional medicine. The continual usage of drugs means that thousands of people in this country are addicts, not because of street-pushed, illegal trafficking, but due to regular treatment prescribed by the doctor. The use of synthetic drugs and other conventional medicine is seen by some as a narrow form of treatment which fails because it doesn't give attention to the whole person: spirit, soul and body. This is something we as Christians should also be interested in. For instance, the Bible's word for salvation carries with it the sense of wholeness. The New Age Movement targets the whole person (a noble aim), but as we've seen in past chapters its perspectives are decidedly occult. It not only offers the standard yoga and meditation, but also the vast and exhaustive range of more recently devised (or repackaged) treatments, some of which, like yoga, have their roots in religion and not science. Acupuncture, past lives therapy, iridology, Reiki, aromatherapy and reflexology form just a small part of the menu.

Many are heralding the rise to popularity of alternative medicine as the most exciting development in the medical arena for years, while others have severe reservations. Why is it that with many of these therapies there appears to be no rational or scientific reason for why they work? Is it that science has not yet discovered the reasons? Is it purely psychological? Or is there some supernatural force at work behind the scenes? It may be that some of these therapies are harmless, but the danger is that they are often bed-mates with clear and overt forms of the occult. For example, the use of pendulum swinging and astrological charts to divine what treatment is required in some (not all) homeopathy, or the use of psychic powers or telepathy to induce healing. I believe that every person must in their own mind have clear answers to these key questions before they consider involvement in these potentially dangerous practices. I can only see this aspect of the New Age Movement mushrooming in the next few years. It has already partially infiltrated the National Health Service as well as having influence across society with people like Prince Charles giving increased credibility to it through their support. Many people who find themselves ill, sometimes terminally (particularly with cancer), will continue to be drawn into these therapies as their hopes of cure under conventional medicine fade away. And who can blame them? Who would want to deny them hope at this tragic phase of their life? Yet, the fact remains, many of them will be drawn, not to the Creator of the universe and to salvation in him, but into the occult at the hands of a misguided New Age therapist.

I remember talking to a young guy in his early twenties called Tim. He had been diagnosed as having a form of cancer which at the time seemed to be responding to conventional treatment. However, in the early days of his illness he decided to take more responsibility for his cure and attended a local cancer help centre, a place renowned for its New Age treatment. He was told that nothing would be offered him that would in any way compromise his Christian faith and so he attended some sessions. It started with dietary instruction and other more neutral treatment, but soon descended into the occult. Yoga and meditation, along with the laying on of hands by a psychic healer were recommended. Teaching sessions were given, particularly emphasising the Eastern concept of reality and the importance of releasing the vital energy in your body. Hindu-style prayer or visualisation was employed to imagine the cancer disappearing from his body. After a short time, Tim realised that as a Christian he could not be involved with these practices and left feeling he'd been deceived by the therapist into taking part in the first place. Alternative medicine, in his case, had nearly been a journey into the occult.

Diet and leisure activities

We live in an age where age is not appreciated! The endless search for eternal youth, fitness and a good physique seems to be a major preoccupation at almost every level of society, particularly among the rich. There is barely a major celebrity these days who hasn't had a face job, nose modification, breast enlargement or reduction, removal of excess fat or bottom pinched (reduced in size, that is!). There are a lot of bionic people about! Clinics of all shapes and sizes exist to help dieting, exercise and other forms of treatment. Some actresses have made millions out of their aerobic tapes, diet books and beauty tips. Much of this is pure vanity, revealing humanity's deep-seated desire to be attractive, popular, needed and accepted. It is a preoccupation with the external, material side of our personality which will never fulfil us at the deepest level. Only God himself is able to fill our spiritual void.

However, there is no virtue in being frumpy and unfit, and some of this emphasis has been helpful in educating the average person into looking after themselves better. In the words of the apostle Paul: 'For physical training is of some value, but godliness has value for all things, holding promise for both the present life and the life to come' (1 Tim. 4:8).

The emphasis upon diet and health has bitten deeply into Western culture and the New Age Movement has been quick to realise this. Again yoga and meditation have made an impression here with herbalism, vegetarianism and all kinds of other techniques high on the agenda. Many health food shops and centres, while being fine in themselves, can act as a centre of New Age propaganda with books on subjects like 'Health and the Stars' being at the front of their displays.

There have also been developments on the side of recreation. Take for example the current craze for the martial arts. Films like *Bullet Proof Monk, Karate Kid* and endless others (see the local video library), have led an army of countless young people karate-chopping into the night! Violence aside, what is the world-view, power and influence behind these Eastern forms of combat and self-defence? That is a question I hope to answer later in this chapter.

Let's now look specifically at some of the practices which characterise the New Age Movement on the ground. Due to a lack of space, this will be brief and by no means exhaustive. However, I hope that what is covered will be helpful.

Information below is taken from *The New Age and You*, Roger Ellis and Andrea Clarke (Kingsway, 1992).

Acupuncture

Thousands of people all over the world are voluntarily allowing themselves to become human pincushions after being impressed by the incredible claims of the ancient art of acupuncture. Needles are inserted into the skin at points on invisible energy channels, called meridians, which are supposedly linked with internal organs. The needles are claimed to be able to unblock, increase or decrease the flow of this energy, or ch'i, when rotated either by hand or by use of an electric current. These meridian lines were first drawn up 5,000 years ago by Huang Ti, the yellow emperor, who combined his belief in astrology and the Taoist Yin/Yang approach to life with his limited knowledge of the functioning of the human body (dissecting the human body was prohibited). There is no proof that these meridians exist, that there is a tangible energy flowing through the body, or that there is a biological link between these points and the internal organs that it's claimed they control. The only scientific evidence for using needles is in the relief of pain where the nerves are able to be blocked from sending signals to the brain.

Acupressure

Instead of needles, pressure is applied to the same meridian points. This is also known as shiatsu massage. The acupressurist may use hands, elbows, knees, or even feet to apply the pressure, along with an assortment of oils and herbal remedies.

Bracelets and bands, which are claimed place pressure on specific energy points on the body and so ease travel sickness or pain from such things as rheumatism, also come under this heading.

Aromatherapy

There is nothing essentially wrong with something that smells nice. Aromatic fragrances can make you feel relaxed, comfortable and at ease. We know that our sense of smell triggers memories – some good, some bad. For instance, we can start to salivate if we smell particularly good food. Aromatherapy involves massaging, bathing and inhaling with essential oils of various herbs. Nothing wrong with that, except that many of the essential oils on the market claim to be made in such a way as to release the vital energy of the original substance, therefore stimulating and enhancing the body's energy.

Biorhythms

Graphs are drawn up, based on a twenty-three-day cycle, for physical vitality, strength, endurance, confidence and sex drive, a twenty-eight-day cycle of emotional moods and creative ability, and a thirty-three-day cycle governing intellectual ability, decision making, memory and learning ability. Based on the individual's date of birth as the start date for these cycles, one is supposed to be able to plot the individual ups and downs of life and therefore make valuable decisions about things such as, 'When is the best time to take a driving test?' or 'How will I be feeling next Tuesday as opposed to last Tuesday?'

Homeopathy

'Like cures like.' Introduced by Samuel Hahnemann (1755–1843), this is perhaps one of the most controversial of the new medicine techniques, not least because it has been made so respectable due to the patronage of the royal family. Now found readily available on the shelves of most high street chemists and health food shops, homeopathic 'natural' products can be prescribed for a plethora of complaints. But on what basis do they work, and are they really as natural as they claim?

Rebelling against the medical profession, Hahnemann began his own research and discovered that when he took quinine he suffered the symptoms associated with malaria. Although in later experiments this same reaction could not be proved, leading to the conclusion that Hahnemann had in fact suffered an allergic reaction to the quinine. He believed that he was able to treat a variety of illnesses using dilutions of substances which in their full strength would cause the same symptoms in a healthy person. He drew up charts which relied heavily on his understanding of Eastern philosophy and his deep interest in the occult and all forms of psychic and paranormal phenomena, and he came to the conclusion that it was in the process of dilution that the power to heal was released from the original substance.

Hahnemann claimed that throughout the stages of dilution as the substance is shaken, a cosmic vital energy force is released, and it is to this 'force' that he attributed the success of his homeopathic remedies. He was particularly keen on a solution so diluted that if tested not even a single molecule of original substance would be found in the bottle of supposed remedy. In short, too little active chemical to do any harm and too little to do any good.

Today, some homeopaths would be reluctant to use quite the same level of dilution that Hahnemann instructed so that their remedies could have some organic effect (although this is very unlikely). And some would openly admit their faith in occult practices, adhering to the idea that there is cosmic vital energy in all things animal, vegetable and mineral and that they are able to release and harness this power for healing.

Homeopathy has been very quickly and easily adopted into the New Age spectrum of treatments, and while it would be comforting to think that it is possible to take natural remedies with little or no physical side effects, until it has been categorically and scientifically proved that cure is rooted in a measurable physical reaction or change within the body, one must assume that the power behind homeopathy is spiritual and has spiritual side effects.

Bach flower remedies are marketed in a very similar way, and you can find small bottles of these remedies in most health food shops. These flower remedies are diluted in solutions of brandy and water and claim to be able to vastly improve, if not cure, conditions such as loneliness, fanatical beliefs, depression and anxiety, as well as a list of physical ailments. How anyone can believe that a few drops of potion will cure the fact that they live alone and have very few friends we are not sure. The potential danger in such cures speaks for itself. 'Cures' which promise miraculous results yet have no real power could prove fatal to those who are desperate.

Hypnotherapy

Used in a variety of treatments from fear of spiders to dentistry, modern hypnotism, pioneered by Franz Mesmer (1734–1815), is still on the increase. Gaining credence with the conventional medical profession as a helpful extra, the patient's conscious mind is put on pause, rather like a video machine, and the subconscious comes 'out to play'. Once in a trance, the patient is able to be manipulated by the hypnotist's suggestions. This only works if the patient is a 'willing victim', completely trusting the hypnotist and allowing him or herself to become like a robot without any control. People have been known to suffer from severe psychological side effects as a result of undergoing hypnosis, and some have been known to experience confusion and personality changes involving uncontrollable laughter, anger and crying.

Mesmer confessed to finding that while he performed his stage act, which involved hypnotising members of the audience, he would find himself overcome by an outside occult power. Hypnotism undoubtedly has many roots in the occult and is an integral part of some witchcraft practices. Many people have claimed to have clairvoyant or psychic experiences as a result of hypnosis, which is similar to a medium's trance.

Hypnotism is an essential part of many New Age practices, including rebirthing in which patients are supposedly able to retrace through their subconscious mind all the stages of their life and before that to past lives, going over supposed events which have moulded and shaped their current personality. Heavily linked with the Eastern philosophy of reincarnation, patients are supposed to be able to talk in different voices and take on other characters as though they were someone else in a past time. We are very clear in our view that these are in fact the same phenomena associated with trance channelling or medium spirits . . .

Some practitioners claim that hypnotism is purely mental and in no way dangerous. One wonders how they are able to justify this against the evidence to the contrary. Laying aside the dangers of the spiritual dimension involved, it is certainly dangerous to allow oneself to be at the mercy of hypnotists, however bona fide they may seem.

Iridology

Studying the markings on the iris of the eyes and observing changes in them, these New Age practitioners claim to be able to locate and diagnose problems in the body and mind. Conventional doctors do look into the eyes to see indications of specific diseases. However, they would not go as far as iridologists who claim that the iris is like a map of the entire body, and little wonder as this has not been proved to be scientifically correct. . . .

Reflexology

To the reflexologist, the foot is the mirror of the body. Parts of the sole are said to be connected, via 'energy channels', to other parts of the body. Dividing up specific areas of the feet to represent the different organs, the reflexologists embark on a course of foot massage to stimulate the flow of this supposed energy and move any of the sedimentation they claim has built up and caused blockages for it. No clinical trials have been conducted to prove the claims made by reflexologists, though they continue to market their technique for a variety of ailments, including back problems, migraine, digestive disorders, period pains and stress.

Vegetarianism

A vegetarian is a person who for one reason or another excludes meat, fish and, if they are 'vegan', egg, milk and cheese from their diet. If you're a vegetarian, rest easy. I'm not going to declare all vegetarianism demonic and yourself unspiritual on the basis of your decision not to eat meat. In the church, there seems to be a genuine confusion as to how to respond to vegetarianism. Views range from, 'How could any Christian kill a poor, innocent, defenceless animal for food?' to 'All vegetarians are into the occult and need deliverance so they can eat meat.' How should we respond to these?

As we have seen earlier, there has been an upsurge of interest in health, diet, exercise and spirituality in the past few years. Eastern thinkers have been quick to recognise this and have marketed their gospel accordingly. Unfortunately, much of the thinking behind the promotion of vegetarianism reflects this. Many Eastern cults (such as Hare Krishna) do not allow the eating of meat as they believe it lowers the spiritual vibrations of people's vital energy and hinders people reaching Brahman or realisation. Similarly, some Buddhists would stand firmly against the killing of all animals (that cow could be your reincarnated granny!) to such a degree that priests in some countries have prevented the killing of rabid dogs, allowing humans to die horribly of rabies as a result. New Agers do not see the distinction between animals and humanity that we observed in Chapter 3. Obviously any vegetarianism, no matter how healthy, if recommended or packaged for these reasons should be abhorrent to the Christian.

However, it does need to be said that there are other reasons given for vegetarianism. It is clear that most Westerners do eat too much red meat and that many illnesses result from an excess of junk food and not enough vegetable roughage. Also, there are some illnesses that can be arrested more quickly if a vegetarian diet is observed. For instance, some doctors believe that the side effects of chemotherapy (cancer treatment) are significantly reduced if the patient observes a vegetarian diet. Also, some people do seem to have a genuine allergy to meat. In the absence of a cure or healing, people should enjoy their preference for vegetarian food, thanking God without any guilt.

What then, in brief, does the Bible say about the eating of meat? Well, as some evangelical vegetarians point out, it is clear that before the Fall recorded in Genesis 3, humanity was wholly vegetarian: 'Then God said, "I give you every seed-bearing plant on the face of the whole earth and every tree that has fruit with seed in it. They will be yours for food"' (Gen. 1:29).

However, the Fall of humanity, the subsequent judgement of the earth and also the judgement at the flood (Gen. 6–8) changed the situation. God brought in a new agreement (covenant) with humanity through Noah. Part of that covenant was that 'Everything that lives and moves will be food for you. Just as I gave you the green plants, I now give you everything' (Gen. 9:3).

Therefore throughout the rest of the Old Testament humanity is recorded as enjoying eating meat in thankfulness to God. Indeed, God himself, on more than one occasion, miraculously provided meat for the whole Israelite community in the desert (Ex. 16:1–13). Proof enough that from God's perspective the eating of meat was wholly kosher!

In the New Testament it is clear that Jesus himself would have eaten meat (lamb at least) as part of the Passover meal and the Bible also records him eating fish on different occasions (inferred in Mt. 14:13–20; also Jn. 21:13). The apostle Peter was taught some important lessons with regard to meat in Acts 10:9–16.

About noon the following day as they were approaching the city, Peter went up on the roof to pray. He became hungry and wanted something to eat, and while the meal was being prepared, he fell into a trance. He saw heaven opened and something like a large sheet being let down to earth by its four corners. It contained all kinds of four-footed animals, as well as reptiles of the earth and birds of the air. Then a voice told him, 'Get up, Peter. Kill and eat.'

'Surely not Lord!' Peter replied. 'I have never eaten anything impure or unclean.'

The voice spoke to him a second time, 'Do not call
anything impure that God has made clean.'

This happened three times, and immediately the sheet
was taken back to heaven.

In this passage, Peter is commanded not only to eat kosher
(ritually clean) meat, but also 'unclean' meat, which the
Gentiles already ate. Clearly the deeper meaning is that
the Gentiles were clean and could be joint recipients of
God's grace with the Jews in God's new community, the
church. However, as a backdrop lies the truth that all meat
is perfectly okay to eat.

What then should be our response to vegetarianism?
The apostle Paul provides the answer, in Romans 14.

Accept him whose faith is weak, without passing judgment on disputable matters. One man's faith allows him
to eat everything, but another man, whose faith is weak,
eats only vegetables. The man who eats everything must
not look down on him who does not, and the man who
does not eat everything must not condemn the man who
does, for God has accepted him. Who are you to judge
someone else's servant? To his own master he stands or
falls. And he will stand, for the Lord is able to make him
stand.

One man considers one day more sacred than another;
another man considers every day alike. Each one should
be fully convinced in his own mind. He who regards one
day as special, does so to the Lord. He who eats meat,
eats to the Lord, for he gives thanks to God; and he who
abstains, does so to the Lord and gives thanks to God.
For none of us lives to himself alone and none of us dies
to himself alone. If we live, we live to the Lord; and if
we die, we die to the Lord. So, whether we live or die,
we belong to the Lord (Rom. 14:1–8).

As one who is in the Lord Jesus, I am fully convinced that no food is unclean in itself. But if anyone regards something as unclean, then for him it is unclean. If your brother is distressed because of what you eat, you are no longer acting in love. Do not by your eating destroy your brother for whom Christ died. Do not allow what you consider good to be spoken of as evil (Rom. 14:14–16).

So whatever you believe about these things keep between yourself and God. Blessed is the man who does not condemn himself by what he approves. But the man who has doubts is condemned if he eats, because his eating is not from faith; and everything that does not come from faith is sin (Rom. 14:22,23).

It is clear that for the Christian vegetarianism is an option, either in the case of illness, allergy, preference or reasons of conscience, but *not* for religious or spiritual reasons. However, the vegetarian must not look down on the person who eats meat. Similarly, the meat eater must respect the conscience and wishes of the vegetarian. My one plea is that as Christians we allow our consciences and preference to be moulded by the Scriptures and our relationship with God himself and not by the pagan attitudes to eating and lifestyle which are rife in society.

Balancing Factors

What are we to say, then? Are all practices which are aligned, however nebulously, with the New Age movement totally demonic and out of order from a biblical perspective? Can it all be written off in one fell swoop? Well, it does need to be said that the sphere of New Age influence overlaps at many points into areas of neutrality as far as world-view and religious significance are concerned. This is apparent in the business, medical and leisure spheres. Within all three areas nobody would dispute that a healthy diet, regular exercise and positive outlook on life are good for our general wellbeing.

More specifically within medicine, the emerging abundance of alternative therapies is rather like a massive box of eggs – most of which are rotten inside. Until you examine them closely and even crack them open you won't be able to separate the few good from the bad. The challenge to the Christian is to avoid compromise while at the same time resisting a 'reds under the bed' paranoia when approaching this issue. It is a serious mistake to assimilate Eastern mysticism into our lifestyle, but it is almost as misguided to embark on a mindless crusade in opposition. The problem is that some Christians are not just anti New Age, they are anti anything new, whether it is in accordance with Scripture or not!

The Martial Arts

Last, but by no means least, in this chapter we will look briefly at the martial arts. Although they are not New Age as such, there are a number of obvious similarities. Firstly, they share the same basic world-view and underlying spirituality, and secondly, their infiltration of the West has occurred in a similar fashion. There are now a vast selection of martial arts on offer ranging from karate, judo and t'ai chi to kung fu. Although many of them interrelate in terms of style and ethos, there appears to be quite a lot of rivalry between different groupings, each type retaining a certain distinctiveness. The Chinese and Japanese martial arts all have their origins in Eastern mysticism, particularly different types of Buddhism (such as Zen). Many of them owe their invention to monks and have great religious significance, although it does seem strange to me that practices as violent and aggressive as karate and kung fu should originate from allegedly peaceful monks. Karate, for instance, reputedly has its origins in the Shaolin Temple under the Zen Buddhist monk Bodhidharma (Daruma to the Japanese and Ta Mo to the Chinese) supposed to be the 28th reincarnation of Buddha himself. He came to the temple from India during the Liang Dynasty (AD 502–557) and spent nine years in meditation. The following quotes from the book *Judo: The Gentle Way*[5] clearly reveal the heart of the martial arts.

> An encounter with Judo is an encounter with an entire ethos in which one is constantly being urged to develop new qualities as a human being . . . These qualities, and the urge to change, are characteristic elements of the Buddhist approach to life.
>
> Buddhism suggests that each of us, were we to unfold our full potential, could be 'Buddhas', enlightened beings, supremely wise to the reality of things . . . Judo therefore has far more than a casual relationship with Buddhism and with meditation, the central 'tool' of Buddhist practice, and has a blood kinship with meditation.
>
> Judo too is about change, about going beyond yourself as you are right now. If, when you make contact with a Dojo [judo exercise hall treated like a temple] you find that you are making contact with something more than a physical art, more than a foreign culture; if you find you are making contact with something that is really Universal: the urge to grow, to discover higher, truer states of being, then without doubt you will have made contact with at least something of the influence and timeless magic of meditation and Buddhism.

---

5 Alan Fromm and Nicholas Soames, *Judo: The Gentle Way* (London: Routledge & Kegan Paul, 1982).

Alongside these quotes, which clearly reveal their nature, the martial arts pragmatically incorporate many Buddhist concepts like the yin and the yang which they would term the hard and the soft. In consequence, karate would mainly be considered hard (linked with the yin) and t'ai chi soft (linked with the yang). Also, many of the positions adopted during combat are drawn from animism and were originally designed to invoke animal spirits. Hence, for example, the positions based on the monkey, snake or gazelle have dubious spiritual connotations.

Peaceful aggression

There is also a further dilemma facing the Christian with an interest in martial arts. Is the teaching of Jesus and the apostles in any way compatible with a sport so directly rooted in aggression and violence? Should a Christian be developing new and ingenious ways of 'duffing up' his fellow man – even if it does increase fitness? However, concern at the violence and aggression goes much further than this. In the past, the Government had attempted to pass legislation restricting the sale of martial arts accessories and banning some of them, including the lethal Ninja 'death stars'. Clearly the current craze, which has been fuelled by films, video, TV and magazines, could contribute to the spiralling violence in society at large. The time has come for Christians to think clearly and avoid compromise. Buddhism, aggressive violence and Christianity simply don't mix.

Chapter 7

Who is the God of Rock and Roll?

For many years, rock and pop music has evoked a variety of reactions from within the Christian church. Some have accepted the genre lock, stock and barrel, while others beat the rock-music-is-of-the-devil drum with an almost missionary zeal. The new Christian is confronted with countless opinions and the added dilemma of relating his new-found faith to the world around him. 'Where should I draw the line?' 'Is the cinema demonic?' 'Should I destroy all my pop CDs?' 'Can I be a committed, uncompromised Christian without becoming a boring religious clone?' This chapter is about more than rock and pop music. Are the creative arts, including the media, films, music and literature, Satan's territory, forbidden ground for the Christian? Or, are we as Christians free to enjoy what's good without taking the bad on board? Stay tuned for a few answers.

Rock's Edge

No one doubts the power of music as a form of communication. Historically, you can learn much about a civilisation by the music, art and literature of its time.

Similarly, in recent history, developments in the rock culture have been a catalyst to wider changes in society. The influence of the hippie movement of the 1960s with its associated music is a prime example. People also tend to identify the songs of a particular period with the events that occurred in their own life at the time. Sky Sports often replay the football goals of a particular year with the songs of the era in the background. In my own life, songs like *I've Been Waiting for a Girl Like You* by Foreigner remind my wife Maggie and me of the sagas of our romance while engaged and she was away at university. A mixed bag of memories if ever there was one! No doubt you have particular songs which bring back certain memories.

Today there can be no doubt about the powerful influence of music. Pop stars raise millions for charity and are often seen close to politicians either campaigning or supporting their stance. The fashion industry rides piggyback with contemporary music and together they dictate the styles and images which will fill our shops, as well as covering the pages of our newspapers and magazines. Music is fashion, communication and big business. It can both reflect and to a certain degree shape the beliefs, attitudes, lifestyles and morality of its consumers. Rock and pop particularly have the ears of a vast section of the populace, and so it is important to have a biblical approach to it as Christians.

Pop stars like Daniel Bedingfield are gifted, cool and are clear about their Christian faith, which I really like. The music is great too! However, some Christians would feel differently about Christians and pop music. As far as they are concerned, rock and pop music are Satan's tools and so any Christian involved is either deceived, compromised or not a Christian at all.

Rock's Friction

Apart from the image, noise and controversy associated with certain rock celebrities, the reservations of many Christians run much deeper. Some have suggested that the roots of rock, because of its beat, lie within the tribal and occult-permeated culture of Africa. People who hold this opinion generally ignore the fact that much rock music originated from gospel roots and not anything occult. Similarly, reservations about the repetitive beat are a little misplaced in the light of the fact that many hymns and most choruses have a clear beat which at times can seem *very* repetitive. It is interesting to note that Wesley's hymns were not based on any established ecclesiastical style of music. They tended to be influenced by the contemporary style of his day, just like many modern hymns are now written and designed for guitar and keyboards and even a DJ and his decks, as opposed to the outdated organ. This is a sign of the church at last being able to relate relevantly to contemporary culture.

Some critics also cite the controversy of backward masking. This is recording messages backwards, so that they only become recognisable if you reverse your turntable. Some groups have allegedly recorded messages of worship to the devil and other blasphemy. Personally, I have severe reservations as to the truth and importance of these allegations.

Firstly, medics appear unable to prove that backward masked messages in any way influence the subconscious. Secondly, I have yet to hear a supposed backward masked message that sounds clear. Most of them sound something like this: 'Blop Splurge rgh ahoo bloop a gurgle.' I am then encouraged by a zealous anti-rock preacher to believe that this is saying, 'Satan is Lord', when in all reality it could just as easily be, 'Pass the lard' or 'Praise the Lord!' In reality, I believe the controversy of backward masking to be an irrelevant sidetrack.

To be honest, I don't have to listen to Marilyn Manson or The Eagles' *Hotel California* backwards to see the occult or hedonistic influences.

Careless sensationalism will not help our reputation as Christians. We must teach people to avoid mindless crusades and to work out for themselves, in the light of Scripture, which music is acceptable and which isn't. I don't believe music generally or any art form can be declared inherently bad.

Some anti-rock proponents would say that Marilyn Manson's music is evil, not just because of what a song is saying, but also because the song is presented in a rock style. Therefore, if a Christian takes a similar style of music and sings of God's love in Jesus Christ, that is still evil because, no matter what the message, it is the music itself that is bad. Personally, I cannot believe how a thinking Christian can arrive at such a daft viewpoint. Generally, these people have collections full of classical records by people like Wagner who, from what I can gather, was totally off his rocker, steeped in the occult and had Hitler as one of his greatest admirers! Unfortunately, we tend to think that what we like is more spiritual or biblical than the things we dislike.

Without the constraint of the Bible and common sense (and the two are by no means mutually exclusive) I would certainly say that opera is totally demonic! All that screeching sounds really painful. Even the sound itself is guaranteed to give me a headache. Friends of mine tell me that opera is wonderful, but all I can say is each to their own. If people don't like rock and pop music, that's fine, it's their preference. Just as some classical music has strong anti-Christian overtones, so does some rock and pop, and we need to be clear about that. However, as I will now briefly explain, I don't believe that any cultural form can be written off as inherently evil.

What About Culture?

Basically, as Christians our view of culture will either enable us creatively and relevantly to communicate God's love to the world, or bind us into irrelevant modes of communication which will more and more make Christianity a thing of the past, rather than a living faith for the present and future. The issue is not what we like or don't like, but rather what the Bible says. However, it is here that a problem arises, namely the problem of being impartial. In times past all sorts of things have been seen as biblical or unbiblical which on reflection were just cultural norms or taboos. For instance, at one time if a woman wore trousers it was considered an affront to God's order and a confusing of the distinctiveness between sexes. Today, we would still want to retain that distinctiveness, but trousers would not be an issue now in most churches.

What is culture?

In a few sentences, culture is:

1. The total of all inherited ideas, beliefs and social behaviour.

2. The total range of activities and ideas of people.

3. A particular civilisation at a particular period.

4. All the artistic and social pursuits, plus the expression and tastes valued by a society or class.

Culture and the Bible

The root of the problem

In Chapter 2 we looked at what some Bible scholars call the Fall of humanity. We saw how wonderful creation in its original form was and how humanity's rebellion against God was such a heavy rap. As a result, just as creation is totally subject to imperfection (e.g. earthquakes and disasters) so humanity, who was made in God's image, has become soiled in every area of his being. Therefore, if culture is a reflection of humanity's creativity, it will reflect all those imperfections, as it surely does. For example, it is a strange contradiction that human beings can use their intellectual and scientific ability to save lives by medicine on the one hand, while at the same time devise daily more ingenious weapons to destroy life on the other!

Despite this, however, it is clear from some Bible passages that the mark of the Creator is still present in some way within his handiwork: 'For since the creation of the world God's invisible qualities – his eternal power and divine nature – have been clearly seen, being understood from what has been made, so that men are without excuse' (Rom. 1:20).

Similarly, the image of God, which we looked at in Chapter 3, is still present within humanity to one degree or another. Therefore, the ingenuity we see around us in music, literature and other creative forms is at the same time both a reflection of God as Creator, and a testimony to the fact that humanity has fallen away from him and needs salvation like never before.

What is our backdrop?

In spite of the Fall, the overwhelming declaration of the Bible is that 'the earth is the Lord's, and everything in it' (Ps. 24:1). The Hebrews never saw the earth or culture as evil, and as a result their world-view was distinct from many of the peoples around them, particularly that of the Greeks, many of whom were Gnostics.

Some Gnostics believed that the material or physical realm was wholly unspiritual and evil (asceticism to all you boffins). Therefore, the enjoyment of things like eating, drinking and music was considered unspiritual, even if there was nothing morally wrong about the entertainment and no drunkenness or gluttony was involved. Only things of the spirit were really good.

Other Gnostics separated the spirit from the flesh in a different way. They maintained that a person could be involved in whatever sin or immorality they liked as long as their spiritual relationship with God was okay (sensualism).

I see elements of both these errors present in the church today. A minority of Christians stand entrenched against the enjoyment of art, music, cinema, food and drink, saying that they are fleshly and soulish. These people often misguidedly obstruct Christians who are using their creative and artistic gifts to glorify God. Others are proper 'pseuds'. They submerge themselves in excesses of every kind, while still maintaining an air of religiosity about them.

The Bible, as we will see, frees us to be involved in contemporary culture and at the same time warns us of the dangers of compromise. One Christian rock musician was asked how Christians could exist in the perverse world of rock and where he drew the line as far as morality is concerned. His answer went something like this, 'Oh, we draw the line at sin!' If only some so-called church leaders would speak with such clarity!

In the Old Testament, the creative arts are certainly not seen as unspiritual. The Holy Spirit himself is seen as present in building (through inspired craftsmen), artistic needlework, clever metalwork, songs, poetry and writing. Worship and religion were never separated from the rest of life. Paul picks up this concept in the New Testament: 'Therefore, I urge you, brothers, in view of God's mercy, to offer your bodies as living sacrifices, holy and pleasing to God – which is your spiritual act of worship' (Rom. 12:1).

True spirituality is expressed through everyday life. Our meetings at church are just the icing on the cake because worship has as much to do with lifestyle as singing. Clearly there is much good to be experienced within human creativity, especially when the authors are influenced by the Holy Spirit.

However, it is at this point in the debate when people generally point out that 'the heart is deceitful above all things' (Jer. 17:9), inferring that because music is creative it is specifically prone to evil. I normally remind them of God's gift to Christians of a new and redeemed heart (Jer. 31:33; Heb. 8:10–12). So, as Christians, we are able to be freed from our past where our creative gifts were often misused. We have a new heart, and so our minds, wills and creativity (although still imperfect) can uniquely express the life of God.

Despite this, some people still secretly feel that music is 'soulish', which of course it is because it involves interplay between our minds, creativity and emotions. However, their meaning of the word soulish is a little broader – they mean it is plain unspiritual! One well-known preacher talked in conversation to me about the dangers of soulish praise. I told him, somewhat sarcastically I confess, that all my praise was 100 per cent soulish. He looked totally bewildered. I then explained that I wasn't into astral travel as my body, mind, emotions and other critical faculties stayed connected to my spirit throughout my worship of God! I hope he saw my point.

So, culture itself is a neutral medium; that is, it is neither good nor bad in and of itself. Music, drama, acting, newspapers, oratory and writing can be used towards both negative and positive ends.

To boldly go . . .

I once heard the story of a couple who prayed earnestly about whether or not they should risk contamination by the world and hire a television. Satisfied that God had answered their prayers, they awaited the delivery of the brand new set. Upon its arrival, they were horrified to find the following advertising on the packaging: 'Hire a television. Bring the world into your home.' Deeply distressed at the threat of becoming worldly, they sent the TV back!

Such misplaced fear of the world at large is sadly characteristic of many Christians. The biblical call is to be in the world but not of it; that is, to be a bold and vital part of the whole of society yet retain our distinctiveness. Unfortunately, some Christians have got it the wrong way round. They are of the world (selfish, materialistic, and so on) but not in it (never rub shoulders with people outside the church). As Christians we should move like chameleons within our culture, only challenging it when it cuts across things *clearly* revealed in Scripture. Our mandate as a church is to overcome the world (1 Jn. 5:4) and possess land for God. Unfortunately, we will never possess any land without first being involved positively as salt within its culture.

> You are the salt of the earth. But if the salt loses its saltiness, how can it be made salty again? It is no longer good for anything, except to be thrown out and trampled by men.
> You are the light of the world. A city on a hill cannot be hidden. Neither do people light a lamp and put it under

a bowl. Instead they put it on its stand, and it gives light
to everyone in the house. In the same way, let your light
shine before men, that they may see your good deeds and
praise your Father in heaven (Mt. 5:13–16).

Watch Your Step

'So, if you think you are standing firm, be careful that you
don't fall!' (1 Cor. 10:12). It is encouraging to know that
we are free to enjoy music and the rest of culture without
condemnation. However, not all of the anti brigade's
perspectives are misplaced. We must be aware of the
abundance of ungodly propaganda existing at almost
every level of culture. To take music as an example, I find
it alarming to see how many Christians take some music
on board without measuring its compatibility to the faith
they profess.

I remember when I first met my wife. She was sixteen
years old, and having been brought up in a Christian home,
was beginning to get to grips with the issue of being a
twentieth-century Christian in the big, wide world. By
contrast, I had not been brought up in a Christian home
and had lived all of my teenage years way outside of God's
purposes, only changing (for the better, I hasten to add)
when I became a Christian at the age of nineteen. Despite
being a bit green in my faith, I was totally flabbergasted
when on our second date she arrived wearing a Black
Sabbath T-shirt she'd been given. Now, I was into heavy
metal, but this was ridiculous! When I asked her how she
balanced up worshipping Jesus while wearing a Black
Sabbath T-shirt she was surprised, having never looked
at it that way. After a little discussion she made a good
decision, condemning the T-shirt to an eternal fate as a
duster!

Don't get me wrong; I don't believe it is right to lay down strict rules of dress so we can proudly say, 'This is what a Christian should look like,' or, 'This is the music all good Christians should listen to.' That would be ridiculous, immature and unbiblical. However, we must all ask questions about the kinds of films, books and music we consume. Soon after I became a Christian, I re-evaluated my record collection, deciding that I didn't want to pay money to, or play the records of, any band who had a totally anti-Christian stand. As a result, my record collection shrunk somewhat. Fortunately, I had plenty of good ones left! We need to understand that if we continually fill our minds with blatantly violent, aggressive or sexist music, we may eventually end up behaving that way. Hence some of the complaints against rappers like Eminem whose lyrics have carried both destructive violent and negative sexual imagery too.

Four Types of Song

Generally speaking, as we begin to look more carefully at the music that is around, we will see four types of song.

1. *Blatantly occult*
Songs with a theme or emphasis that is drenched in the occult. In my opinion, no Christian can remain fully true to his faith while buying or listening to such records. However, I am not advocating that we bash new Christians over the head with this. Rather, we should gently and reasonably help them to understand the truth and respond to it.

2. *Immoral*
Songs reflecting a lifestyle or attitude that cuts right across Christian values. Many pop songs are sexually

promiscuous. My hope is that most people do not take the lyrics of these songs too seriously. However, if taken seriously the view of some of these songs could lure people towards ruining their lives sexually. This leads them further away from God's good purposes for their lives.

3. Songs reflecting human experience

Music portraying joy, love, disappointment or pain – experiences that are common to all of us. Many songs are about the experience of being in love, for example. Such songs contain a harmless message and can be enjoyed with no problem – that is, if you like the music.

4. Songs with a Christian perspective

These are generally only a threat if you are running from God!

What About Image?

As I have already said, the fashion world rides piggyback with the music industry and together they set many of the trends in dress, hairstyle and image. How should we as Christians respond to this? Some would say that all men should have short back and sides and wear a suit at all times. Women, of course, should look like they've come from Frumpsville, Arizona wearing the usual line in wraparound skirts, floppy jumpers, sandals and, of course, a headscarf. Such dress is considered Christ-like!

I often feel that if Jesus appeared in the church wearing the same gear as he did in biblical times we would be a little surprised. Jesus and the disciples clearly wore the clothes that were common to their day. Similarly, we should not be afraid to deck ourselves out with clothes that are fashionable. To imply that it is more spiritual to look miserable, dowdy and out-of-date is another form of Gnosticism. On the other hand, however, trendy people are certainly not superior in any way to those who are more conservative. Remember, God doesn't judge us by our outward appearance but by our hearts. I sometimes wish people outside the church were like this. However, when they see the street witness full of people dressed like they are time warped, it tends to put them off the message before they've even heard it. A common response would be, 'If Christianity makes you look like that I think I'll give it a miss!'

Some advice

Fashion designers are making statements; statements about things like creativity, music, morality, politics and sexuality. Our clothes therefore communicate, and so as Christians we will need to evaluate our dress to ensure that we are not making an unintended impression. Work it out for yourself. What is the dividing line between:

1. Looking attractive and giving a sexual green light?

2. A statement of individuality and a statement of anarchy and rebellion?

3. Fashionable jewellery and occult symbolism?

4. Looking different and merging your identity too closely with the opposite sex?

Earrings for example

A frantic Christian leader phoned a friend of mine wanting to speak to him urgently. My friend rushed to the phone wondering what terrible problem he may be faced with. 'It's my son,' said the caller. He paused, leaving my friend to wonder, 'Has he been involved in an accident, lost his faith, or become ensnared in some kind of dreadful sin?' After the pause, the caller plucked up courage and with despair blurted, 'He's wearing an earring!' My friend, trying to control his amusement, assured him that there was nothing to worry about. After all, things could be worse!

I have heard many things said against earrings. These have ranged from the fact that they are demonic, worldly and a sign of slavery to Satan, right through to the assertion that they are okay for women, but are too feminine for men. What does the Bible say about them? Well, earrings are frequently mentioned in the Old Testament, as are nose rings which are also in fashion today in some circles. Sometimes they were regarded as talismans or amulets (see Chapter 4), but at other times they were purely a form of decorative jewellery. In the time of Moses it seems that at least on this occasion they were worn by both sexes (see Ex. 32:2). The Bible obviously doesn't see them as inherently evil as this verse in Proverbs points out: 'Like an earring of gold or an ornament of fine gold is a wise man's rebuke to a listening ear' (Prov. 25:12).

I believe, therefore, that it's perfectly okay to wear earrings and nose rings provided there is no occult symbolism involved. Personally, I've decided not to wear an earring because my wife doesn't like them! However, another of the leaders in our church wears an earring, but retains a sensitivity to people in other churches who wouldn't appreciate it. So, sometimes when he goes to lead worship elsewhere, he will remove his earring first. After all, it's hardly worth falling out with fellow Christians over a stupid earring! As far as body piercing is concerned, rather like vegetarianism, I believe it's down to conscience. It really depends which parts of our body we are having pierced, and whether the piercing is a helpful and positive statement about our humanity/sexuality and faith or represents an attitude which hinders growth in God and sends confusing messages about our faith to others.

Don't be taken in

Creative arts always reflect the spiritual state of their originators. If a musician is either far away from God, a manic-depressive or a strong believer, the chances are that this will be fully reflected in their music. By this I mean not just in the lyrical content but also in the 'feel', atmosphere or spirit of the music. As Christians, we must be careful to use discernment, and not be conformed to the image of the music we listen to but to Jesus Christ: 'Do not conform any longer to the pattern of this world, but be transformed by the renewing of your mind. Then you will be able to test and approve what God's will is – his good, pleasing and perfect will' (Rom. 12:2).

When my wife Maggie was studying for her A levels, much of her work involved the reading and understanding of poetry and literature which had a particularly negative, pessimistic and suicidal feel. She found that unless she exercised self-control, the moods or spirit behind the literature would begin to affect her, making her depressed.

Some rock music is like this, the Pink Floyd album, *The Wall*, being a prime example. Despite the fine musicianship, its cynicism, hopelessness and negativism make it a guaranteed party stopper. We need to be aware of the messages being portrayed behind the music.

Christians on the front line

Bono, The Edge and Larry Mullen Jr from the band U2, Daniel Bedingfield, Stacey Oricco and many others have made it big in the music scene. Still others have a belief in God or are close to faith. How should we react to them?

Some Christians seem to snipe at every opportunity, while others worship from afar. Well, we certainly don't have to agree with everything they do, nor do we have to like their music. However, I believe we must honour them for their Christian stand. If from time to time they make mistakes, we must pray for their protection and covering, realising that we are not perfect either. We need to support them, and pray for their spiritual wellbeing and continued success. Armchair criticism is not exactly a fruit of the Spirit.

By the Way – What About Video?

Within the pop charts these days a video or DVD can make or break a song. It can dramatise the lyrical content, represent the feel of the music or add a whole new dimension to it. It is well worth asking yourself what kind of message is being portrayed by a video. Many are just plain fun and totally harmless, while others carry subtle messages. The effect of pop videos, however, is negligible compared to the success of the video/DVD hire shops.

Alongside many spiritually questionable films there are loads of others that, in my opinion, make great viewing. Films like *Billy Elliot, The Matrix* and *Lord of the Rings* make for a great evening's entertainment. Some tackle challenging themes and it's always a challenge to think, pray and ask God what we can learn from them. Almost 100 per cent of all actors, film directors and scriptwriters do not profess Christianity. Also, most films are about people who are not Christians. As a result their content is hardly going to be 100 per cent biblical! However, films offer us a 'snapshot', a window to understand what is happening in our society. It's just like reading the paper, watching TV or being with friends from work, school or college. Therefore, for example, a certain amount of swearing would not deter me personally from watching a film that apart from that is good entertainment. You can't expect Eddie Murphy or Chris Rock to say 'Oh dear' when confronted by a crisis situation! However, I would never choose such language myself, nor would I watch a film which is full of blasphemy and profanity.

Similarly with violence. In some films (like, for example, *Saving Private Ryan*) it could be argued that the violence is justifiable as it makes a point against violence, portraying either actual events that took place or the catastrophic effects of war. On the other hand, I find the violence and murder depicted in some movies excessive, provocative and unnecessary. Many Christians complain of fears of violence, rape, death, the dark and the occult, yet continue to watch videos filled with them! One bloke, who lived with us for a while, had been so frightened by horror videos and books that he couldn't turn his bedroom light off at night. My advice for him, and indeed for all Christians, is: avoid all gratuitously violent, horror-filled and occult-based movies and allow God to deliver you from all your fears (Ps. 34:4).

On this issue it is impossible to draw strict guidelines. We must learn to discern for ourselves and have the guts to turn off any film which unexpectedly takes a turn for the worse. If the film is being shown by friends who are not Christians perhaps a *polite* withdrawal from the situation is in order. Personally, I would rather fear God than other people.

The Bible doesn't give us the option of escape from the world using prohibition-style edicts against music and other art forms. We are to be in the world but not of it. The answer to my question: 'Who's the God rock and roll?' is therefore: 'It depends upon the rocker!'

It is impossible to cover all the issues involved in culture, fashion and dress in a few paragraphs. However, I hope the things I've said, along with my approach to these issues, will help you to come to your own conclusions.

Chapter 8

Satan's Stranglehold – A Way Out

Do you know your birth sign?
Do you follow the stars?
Believing in bad luck and superstition.
Predictions in your horoscope
Beginning to come true.
Without it you don't want to make decisions.
No one knows the future so don't believe the lie,
Astrologers are tools in Satan's hands.
Ouija boards and tarot cards
Are more than harmless fun:
They are the doorway that will lead you
To destruction.

Come into my parlour, says the spider to the fly.
There are many pleasures, do you wanna try?
But a welcome turns to terror
And the Devil sucks you dry.
Demons feeding on your soul;
Their laughter drowns your cry.
Is anybody there? Is anybody there?
Is anybody there?
Does anybody care?

A séance looks inviting,
A little harmless fun.

Dim the lights, hold hands and concentrate.
See! The glass is moving,
Spelling out a name.
Messages from far beyond the grave.
Suddenly it's frightening, out of control.
The smiles are gone as evil moves the hands.
Hearts are beating faster,
Fear fills the gloom.
Spirits from the twilight
Take command.

Evil spirits hide behind
A mask of innocence,
Enticing you with every word they say.
Getting deeper into witchcraft,
Believing in the lie,
That reality is but a step away.
The road on which you're trav'ling leads you to a
living hell
Where thousands cry in torment for release.
The kiss of death will not be sweet;
It is the final act,
That consummates your marriage
To the beast.[6]

People rarely jump straight into the deep end of the occult. Involvement can start with anything from an unhealthy interest in superstition, through to taking part in a seemingly harmless game. The slope then becomes steeper, more slippery and the descent increasingly frightening. The lyrics of this song by Noel Richards dispel the deceptive mist which covers the occult, exposing the real dangers to the clear light of day. This chapter will

---

[6] *Is Anybody There?* By Noel Richards © Kingsway's Thankyou Music 1988.

look at some of the awful consequences of occult involvement, as well as plotting a clear course to freedom from its influence.

Welcome To Your Nightmare

We live in a society used to instant responses, a pushbutton society. Our consumer mentality means that when we press the remote control on the TV we expect to see the screen immediately burst into life in obedience to our command. If not, repairs would be in order! Technology is at our beck and call, operating to provide us with all kinds of information and entertainment. We, however, are in the driving seat.

Sadly, many people approach the powers of darkness with this kind of attitude. Whether it is Ouija, astrology, tarot or witchcraft, people genuinely believe that the powers behind these practices can be manipulated by us with no cost, just like the TV screen. Spiritual powers can be played with like a computer game. If you become discontented, just turn the screen off and you need never use the game again; it is your choice. Such an approach is dangerously misplaced.

Unfortunately, occult spiritual forces are not like machines under our control. They are powerful spirit beings ruled by the prince of darkness, Satan himself (see Chapter 3). They have both personality (albeit twisted) and power to inflict great damage upon people who stand outside of God's protection.

For every journey into the occult there is a price to pay. Try to manipulate or control Satan and the reverse may occur. You begin to be manipulated and controlled by him, but with one difference; Satan never sleeps, he cannot be turned off like a computer screen. The occult is neither a game, a dream, nor is it like a fictional horror movie which finishes as the television is turned off.

As many have discovered, dabbling can be the start of a journey into your own real-life nightmare.

The Thumbs Down

In contrast to what you would perhaps expect, it is by no means just church leaders who are speaking out about the dangers of the occult. Many psychiatrists, who would not appear to be particularly Christian, warn about the damage to the mind that occult involvement brings. On top of this, those within the medical profession who are also Christian have observed both the spiritual as well as the mental and physical problems that exist.

The following quotes from Christian doctors and psychiatrists have been taken from the handout *Doorways to Danger* produced by the Evangelical Alliance.[7]

Psychiatrist Chris Andrew warns: 'Involvement with the occult can lead to anything from depression and broken relationships to sexual deviation and murder.' Even those who become involved in astrology, séances and spells for fun risk 'devastating consequences' says former senior consultant to the Royal Liverpool Hospital and University of Liverpool, Dr David Enoch. 'They're unleashing forces into the lives that they don't understand and often cannot combat.'

Consultant psychiatrist Dr Stewart Checkley says: 'I have seen patients whose involvement with relatively minor forms of the occult has caused them to suffer mental illness. I have seen someone who, as a result of

---

[7] Available from EA.

one experiment with a Ouija board, suffered frightening experiences outside of his control, including automatic handwriting. He found himself writing frightening messages to himself.'

Dr Checkley concludes, 'Such things as Ouija boards and tarot cards can definitely harm. They open up the mind to outside forces.'

A host of medical experts support this view. Dr Roger Moss, a consultant psychiatrist asserts: 'People's mental state can be seriously affected by contact with the occult, particularly among the vulnerable.' Psychiatrist Dr Chris Andrew agrees that any involvement in the occult is dangerous, saying: 'There is a risk of mental and spiritual disease at every possible level.'

To such medical opinion is added the full weight of the Christian Medical Fellowship. Declares a former secretary, Dr Keith Saunders: 'I am in touch with 20,000 doctors around the world who would say there is no doubt that involvement with spirits other than the Holy Spirit will lead to suffering in body, mind and spirit.'

Biblically Speaking

Many so-called contemporary thinkers have maligned the Scriptures saying that those who lived two thousand years ago had a superstitious outlook on life. As a result they supposedly blamed the devil and evil spirits for all kinds of unexplained illnesses and behaviour. While this assertion may be true of the hyper-superstitious Middle Ages, it certainly does not hold true when applied to New Testament times. It is incorrect on at least two counts. Firstly, in the New Testament there was often a clear differentiation between illnesses and behaviour that were demonic on the one hand, and those that were not, on the other.

In the book of Matthew we are told that people brought to Jesus 'all who were ill with various diseases, those suffering severe pain, the demon-possessed, the epileptics and the paralytics, and he healed them' (Mt. 4:24b). Like many modern-day medics, the disciples clearly learned that *some* complaints were a direct result of demonic infiltration.

Secondly, the advent of the scientific age has failed to eradicate concrete experiences of demonic power and possession as illustrated by the experience of church leaders, doctors and many ordinary people who have been faced with occult phenomena. In the face of this, the New Testament is far from ignorant and superstitious. In fact it is relevant, accurate and true to real life experiences.

Demons afflict people

The stories of people who have suffered as a result of occult involvement are given a sharp focus through the teaching of the New Testament. Evil spirits (otherwise called demons or unclean spirits) are seen working in many different ways in the lives of human beings. The table below shows a few examples. It is clear from these examples that demons have the power to influence people in ways ranging from extreme behavioural problems, like anger and violence, through to physical sickness. Notice that in each case, to some extent, people have actually become enslaved by demonic powers.

Passage	Symptom(s)
Matthew 12:22–23	Blindness and dumbness.
Mark 5:1–13	Madness, suicidal tendencies, self-abuse, uncontrollable behaviour, personality corrupted and changed, evil spirit speaks through the person (direct voice), unusual strength displayed in conflict situations.

Passage	Symptom(s)
Luke 9:37–43a	Fits and convulsions resembling epilepsy.
Acts 16:16–19	Possession of psychic powers: in this instance fortune telling.

I am by no means suggesting that all sickness and misfortune are due to the presence of evil spirits. However, it is abundantly clear that some are.

What is Possession?

The statement often made that a person is possessed is not always understood correctly. The word is often interpreted in terms of ownership, which would be its meaning in contemporary language. However, the New Testament word means to be afflicted, influenced, tormented or controlled, rather than to be owned.

The Bible is clear that all those who refuse to believe in Jesus and oppose him are in one sense owned by the devil (Jn. 8:44). By contrast, those who have given their lives to Jesus Christ are now under God's ownership and have become his possession (Eph. 1:14; 1 Cor. 6:19, 20).

However, some Christians forget that being a believer in Jesus by no means provides an automatic exemption from demonic influence and infiltration. That is why we are encouraged to be on the lookout, prepared for the devil's attacks: 'Be self-controlled and alert. Your enemy the devil prowls around like a roaring lion looking for someone to devour. Resist him, standing firm in the faith, because you know that your brothers throughout the world are undergoing the same kind of sufferings' (1 Pet. 5:8, 9).

Any Christian who, either in the past, present or future, opens himself to Satan's attacks without resisting can come under the influence of evil spirits.

The table below briefly outlines some examples of believers in the Bible who were troubled by demonic infiltration.

Name and Identity	Passage	Description
Ananias and Sapphira Part of the Jerusalem church.	Acts 5	Verse 3 declares that Satan has 'filled' the heart of Ananias.
Judas Iscariot A disciple and believer (Mk. 3:19; Mt. 10) who was sent out with the others. He was clearly one of the disciples (Acts 1:17).	John 13:27	Although a believer, Judas gave himself over to the evil of betraying Jesus, and Satan 'entered' him.
Peter – The Disciple	Matthew 16:23	Whether Peter was possessed for a time is not clear. However, he was certainly influenced by Satan in a similar way that God had influenced him in Matthew 16:16, 17.

And there are other examples which we have no space to cover here.

The Bible seems to take for granted the fact that Satan is a predator looking for easy prey. As such he is not choosy and will mercilessly attack both Christian and non-Christian alike in any way he can. However, the thrust of the gospel message is good news. We are not left without guidance concerning the path to freedom. The New Testament shows us the way, in Jesus Christ, both through its teaching and the documentation of the real life experiences of ordinary people (such as Mary Magdalene in Lk. 8:1–3).

It is clear from a practical observation of society that occult phenomena are widespread. We have the testimony of many medics as well as individual people whose lives have been messed up. Demonic attack could almost be considered one of the greatest dangers and hazards we could face in life. What I now want to do is look at some of the main ways in which people open themselves to demonic infiltration.

1. Occult

Say no more! I think I have already emphasised enough the dangers of occult involvement.

2. The sin ladder

The effectiveness of any machine's performance is dependent on it being in an environment which is compatible with its prominent characteristics. For example, a sports car operates superbly when used on well-made roads, but try and take it into fields and through rivers and you will soon wreck it. On the other hand, a tank is not really suitable for commuting to work, but is really in its element on rough terrain.

The Bible shows us two types of terrain. Within one, Satan is fully at home and works for the destruction of all who trespass there. In the other, the Holy Spirit operates freely to strengthen and enrich people.

(a) Satan's territory: 'The acts of the sinful nature are obvious: sexual immorality, impurity and debauchery; idolatry and witchcraft; hatred, discord, jealousy, fits of

rage, selfish ambition, dissensions, factions and envy; drunkenness, orgies, and the like. I warn you, as I did before, that those who live like this will not inherit the kingdom of God' (Gal. 5:19–21).

(b) The Holy Spirit's territory: 'But the fruit of the Spirit is love, joy, peace, patience, kindness, goodness, faithfulness, gentleness and self-control. Against such things there is no law' (Gal. 5:22, 23).

When we are within God's territory we are safe. It is where we have been created to live. The Holy Spirit, like a fruit with nine flavours, each designed to bring happiness and contentment.

The other territory stands in stark contrast. It is not just full of the occult, but also all behaviour that falls short of God's perfect character (sin). When we persistently and knowingly give ourselves over to sin we are firmly in Satan's territory and as such are particularly vulnerable to demonic influence. This is not to say, of course, that in every case of sin a person is infiltrated by demonic forces. However, persistent sin can open the door to demons as illustrated by the ladder diagram below.

The Sin Ladder[8]

6		Area of life controlled by demonic forces
5		Addiction produces a spiritual void
4		Loss of self-control. Area of life fertile ground for Satan's influence
3		Sin becomes a habit (addictive)
2		Giving in to temptation (sin)
1		Temptation (not sin)

---

[8] Based on an idea by Mike Costello.

In the diagram we can see that it is mainly by progressive, wilful and habitual sin that Satan is able to gain a hold in someone's life.

Temptation itself is not a sin. One great Christian leader once said: 'You can't stop birds flying over your head, but you can stop them nesting in your hair.' So it is with temptation. We are all tempted in many different situations, and in itself temptation is a normal experience and not sinful. The Bible itself states that even Jesus Christ was tempted in every way, just as we are, yet was without sin (Heb. 4:15). Therefore, temptation only becomes sin when we give in to it and are wilfully involved in sin.

Even at this stage, the problem can be clearly dealt with if we confess our wrongdoing to God and be prepared to turn from it: 'If we confess our sins, he is faithful and just and will forgive us our sins and purify us from all unrighteousness' (1 Jn. 1:9). However, if we ignore the way out which God has provided, there is only one way forward and that is deeper into trouble!

Take, for example, the issue of anger (it could just as easily be lust or lying). A person may initially find himself tempted towards anger – which would be normal. However, once yielded to on a continual basis, anger begins to become habitual to such a degree that the person's thinking and reactions in relationships become dominated by anger. It becomes an uncontrolled passion, finding expression through fractured relationships, aggressive impulses, hatred, bitterness, envy and perhaps even physical violence. It is at this stage of uncontrollable, habitual anger that Satan is able to gain access and assume control, tormenting the person endlessly through his weak point of anger. The person has wilfully handed himself over to anger on an ongoing basis and in this context Satan will gladly take ground in a person's life.

Sin is physically, emotionally and spiritually dangerous, not just because it severs our communication lines with God (Ps. 66:18), but also because it leaves us vulnerable to Satan's attacks.

Heredity

'The fathers have eaten sour grapes, and the children's teeth are set on edge' (Jer. 31:29) This is a biblical proverb which basically means the consequences for the sins of people further back in our family line can also affect us now. This is particularly how things stood before Christ under the Old Covenant. The following verse from the Old Testament is part of the first commandment prohibiting idolatry and all forms of the occult: 'You shall not bow down to them or worship them; for I, the LORD your God, am a jealous God, punishing the children for the sin of the fathers to the third and fourth generation of those who hate me' (Deut. 5:9). However, under the New Covenant this proverb should no longer apply because everyone will be accountable for his or her own sin and not the sin of others within their family (Jer. 31:30; Ezek. 18:1–32). Nevertheless, it is still quite common to find Christians who are not living in the fullness of this freedom from their ancestry. Satan is a usurper and wherever possible maintains his hold on a person's life until challenged. Therefore, the occult involvement in the past generations of a person's family can hinder their walk with God now. This seems to be an even more common phenomenon in the lives of people who express no Christian commitment as such.

For example, I have often talked with people who have complained of psychic phenomena and telepathic gifts and yet they have never personally been involved with the occult. Generally, a conversation will reveal that either their parents, an uncle or aunt or someone else in their ancestry was a spiritualist or involved in some other form of the occult. Clearly, there was some way in which Satan had maintained his influence on that family from generation to generation. That is, until the chain was broken by the prayers of a Christian.

Other people have complained of paranoid fears, mental problems or unexplained sicknesses. Sometimes these too can be traced back to occult involvement by a relative (usually no further than three or four generations back – see Deut. 5:9) which has brought a curse upon their family. It is important, therefore, that if we know of any such involvement in our family we should have the spiritual links broken through prayer. This will enable us to grow fully in our Christian life.

Traumatic experience

Another route by which people sometimes find themselves bound up by demonic forces is that of traumatic experience. I have often talked with people who as a result of a particularly disturbing event are permanently scarred both emotionally and spiritually.

It needs to be said again that by no means everybody who encounters trauma in whatever form will fall under demonic influence. For some the need will be a healing of the mind and emotions. However, in certain situations the distress experienced can provide open ground for the enemy to get hold of a person while they are vulnerable.

An example of this would be a young child being locked, perhaps accidentally, in a small dark cupboard for a long period. During this time fears of the dark, suffocation and loneliness can easily develop. I remember praying for one girl who had experienced this. She had become paranoid about the dark, her character changing from that of a happy-go-lucky girl into a person racked by fear at every level. It was only after Satan's hold over this area of fear had been broken (through prayer) that she experienced total freedom and was able to resume normal life.

Freedom: Two Sides to the Deal

1. *Our part: make your mind up time!*

From the things we observed in Chapters 3 and 4, it is clear that God himself has ample power to release those who have become entangled by the powers of darkness. We will explore this further when looking at God's part of the freedom that is available to all those who respond to his truth.

However, there is another side to the coin. God has given each person the free will to choose *for* him or *against* him in every aspect of his life. Therefore, God is not going to force his freedom upon you if you do not want wholeheartedly to be free.

One example of this was when I had a person come to me seeking deliverance from horrifying nightmares and poltergeist-type experiences in her home. I explained that deliverance could only come if she was prepared to recognise her own occult involvement as sin and renounce it totally, along with her psychic powers.

Unfortunately, she was not prepared to do this and as a result I was unable to pray for her release. God has given Christians authority in Christ over Satan's power, but we have no authority to force people into choosing freedom in Jesus Christ. It is entirely up to them.

Our ability to decide for God is often seriously impaired at a number of levels.

Some stand deceived, secure in their bondage to occult powers. 'Better the devil you know' is their motto. It would take a crisis event or a dramatic encounter with the living God to convince them otherwise.

Others have become totally locked up to passivity, either through crippling apathy or due to the fact that their mind has been inoculated against wilful decision by either drugs or Eastern religion. Active decisions are now alien to their character and are therefore difficult to contemplate. Therefore they sit on the fence, never deciding to turn towards Jesus Christ.

It is also true for some that they have been so crushed, hurt and dominated by people and situations that the prospect of handing their life over to God, and the associated freedom that comes with it, is very daunting.

Alongside this, some others are just plain rebellious. They want to live life their own way without any spiritual or moral constraints. They refuse point blank to submit themselves to God's authority. Although ensnared by all sorts of destructive habits they have become happy in this imprisonment. This stance is tantamount to moving headlong towards destruction with their fingers in their ears blocking out the warnings God sends their way. This rebellion will undoubtedly lead them deeper into the occult snare with all its associated dangers.

The key element in us fulfilling our side of the deal is the aligning of our wills, minds and priorities with those of God. This can be done by a threefold process:

(a) Confession. Occult involvement and general wrongdoing must be recognised as sin and confessed (spoken out) openly to God. It is generally advisable to do this out loud in the presence of another Christian: 'Therefore confess your sins to each other and pray for each other so that you may be healed. The prayer of a righteous man is powerful and effective' (Jas. 5:16).

(b) Repentance and renunciation. Repentance is not sentiment, neither is it merely feeling sorry that things have turned out badly. It involves both a change of mind and

direction. Not only does a person have to now see things God's way, but he also has to change his life around to reflect this.

Alongside repentance, renunciation is often necessary. This is when as we say sorry to God (out loud!) we also publicly lay aside our previous behaviour. This is sometimes also necessary when dealing with heredity and traumatic issues. It is often helpful for people to declare out loud that they no longer want to be dogged by a particular problem This profession is a powerful witness which opens wide the way for God's power to come and bring total release.

If a sincere will to stage an about turn (repent) is not present, release from demonic bondage may turn out to be purely surface. For example, if a person is delivered from a problem with lust and still continues to read pornographic literature he will soon have his lust problem back. In fact, according to the Bible, it may well become worse.

> When an evil spirit comes out of a man, it goes through arid places seeking rest and does not find it. Then it says, 'I will return to the house I left.' When it arrives, it finds the house unoccupied, swept clean and put in order. Then it goes and takes with it seven other spirits more wicked than itself, and they go in and live there. And the final condition of that man is worse than the first. That is how it will be with this wicked generation (Mt. 12:43–45).

In these verses Jesus teaches that after prayer a person's life (the house) is swept clean and put in order. However, that person's life needs to be filled with the Holy Spirit and the positive things of God. He needs not only to have turned away from his old life, but also to be committed to God's way of living. If this does not happen, more evil spirits may return to fill the vacuum created by half-hearted repentance. The person may then end up worse off than before. True repentance, therefore, is of vital importance.

(c) Forgiveness. 'Forgive us our sins, for we also forgive everyone who sins against us' (Lk. 11:4). It is clear from this teaching by Jesus that our receiving God's forgiveness is linked directly with our willingness to forgive those who have wronged us.

Jesus was once asked by an inquisitive disciple whether seven was a reasonable number of times to forgive a person who wrongs someone else. He replied that seventy-seven times was more like the number (Mt. 18:21, 22). To the Jewish mind seven was the perfect number and so seventy (or seventy times seven) stands for unlimited forgiveness.

God is not without compassion for people who have been hurt by others. On the contrary, his love is upon all the wounded and oppressed. However, in the light of his unconditional love and forgiveness towards us (in spite of our imperfections) we are required to forgive others without qualification.

In this context, forgiveness is similar to repentance. It too is not a feeling, though feelings may be involved, but an act of the will. We all have the power to forgive, and if we refuse to do so, a spiritual block is created in our lives. While enslaved to unforgiveness it is very difficult, if not impossible, to receive release from demonic oppression.

God is committed to releasing the person who has fallen under Satan's influence. Our only task is to desire God's freedom and to open ourselves up to his power by clearly deciding to do things his way. By clear confession, repentance, renunciation and forgiveness we remove any blockages out of the way.

2. *God's part: releasing the captives*
It is a good job that God hasn't left humanity alone and helpless, struggling in vain against supernatural powers.

If that was the case we would all be forced to give up and become slaves of the enemy. As Christians we can be ever thankful that God is all-powerful and has thoroughly defeated all the powers of darkness (see Chapter 3).

Jesus Christ is humanity's Saviour and Liberator. The whole purpose of his coming was to proclaim salvation, which includes freedom from all demonic oppression: 'The Spirit of the Lord is on me, because he has anointed me to preach good news to the poor. He has sent me to proclaim freedom for the prisoners and recovery of sight for the blind, to release the oppressed, to proclaim the year of the Lord's favour' (Lk. 4:18, 19).

Jesus Christ clearly revealed that one aspect of the good news (gospel) was release from Satan's clutches. The preaching of God's kingdom was synonymous with physical healing and deliverance from evil powers (Mt. 4:23, 24). Whenever freedom from evil is experienced through God's power, then the kingdom of God is advancing (Mt. 12:28).

It is clear from the New Testament that every Christian has been rescued from the kingdom of darkness and brought into God's kingdom. As a result, when Satan attacks the Christian he is on very thin ice, having no real legitimate right to do so. However, his attacks will continue until the Christian realises this and learns to stand firm in prayer: 'Submit yourselves, then, to God. Resist the devil, and he will flee from you' (Jas. 4:7).

Jesus displayed through his ministry that authority over evil spirits was not just to be exercised by him. While he remains the source of all real authority, it is clear from passages like Luke chapters 9 and 10, that authority is also conferred upon his followers or disciples. In Luke 10 particularly, Jesus sends out 70 (or 72) disciples. Again this number has great symbolic significance to the Jewish mind. It stands for the seventy nations of the whole world talked of in Genesis 10. Through this symbolic 70 Jesus is saying that the gospel message is destined not just for the Jews but for all nations.

The 70 disciples were representatives of every nationality, tribe and tongue who would come to faith through the church. These disciples would not just share the gospel message, but would also have potential to move in this authority over Satan.

> He said to them, 'Go into all the world and preach the good news to all creation. Whoever believes and is baptised will be saved, but whoever does not believe will be condemned. And these signs will accompany those who believe: In my name they will drive out demons; they will speak in new tongues; they will pick up snakes with their hands; and when they drink deadly poison, it will not hurt them at all; they will place their hands on sick people, and they will get well.' After the Lord Jesus had spoken to them, he was taken up into heaven and he sat at the right hand of God (Mk. 16:15–19).

Those in the New Testament church were quick to realise their authority. Once the initial penny dropped at Pentecost, it is clear that many people joined their number and in the process were set free from occult influence (see Acts 5:16, 8:7). We can see from this that as Christians we are far from powerless in the face of occult phenomena. We have been given the victory over such things in Jesus Christ.

Coping With Trouble: The Dos and Don'ts

Here are some practical guidelines for people who are either helping someone else, or are personally seeking release in a particular area of their life

The don'ts

1. Never panic, get over excited or melodramatic when in, or confronted by, a situation.

2. Don't move into prayer against evil spirits late at night. The problem is best bound up (Mt. 18:18) in prayer and then dealt with in the cold light of day.

3. Don't pray for a person with an occult problem alone. Never bite off more than you can chew. (Acts 19:11–19). Don't react out of fear, but act in faith.

4. Don't fall into paranoid self-analysis where every problem is seen as demonic. When in this state your judgement will be impaired. If in doubt seek the advice of a mature, spiritually-minded Christian.

The dos

1. Do, when in difficulty, open yourself up for prayer. Follow the guidelines I've already given with regard to aligning your life with God's will.

2. Seek the advice and help (prayers) of a mature Christian who has experience in this area. Learn from this Christian, and from prayer and Bible study how to pray in authority yourself.

3. Learn to be secure in God's promises. Always remember he has won the victory. See things from his perspective and should you find yourself in a frightening situation, trust that he has the ability to see you through it.

4. Grow in faith to the level where you can personally stand your ground against the enemy (Eph. 6:10, 11).

When occult problems are clearly dealt with, it is *then* possible to enjoy the full measure of God's blessing. However, if these problems remain undealt with, lives will be continually affected and our spiritual growth seriously stunted.

Once we have received prayer, it is then important to learn to walk in our freedom. This is a process by which our deliverance, secured the instant the enemy was sent packing, becomes real in our everyday experience. Some find that all the old habit patterns are instantly broken. Others have to learn to walk free through the care of other Christians, soaking in the Bible's teaching, and most importantly developing a stronger relationship with the Lord Jesus himself. As this is done, a complete transformation is experienced throughout our minds, emotions and lifestyle. We must be encouraged by the fact that once God has started something in a life, he is committed to finishing it: '. . . being confident of this, that he who began a good work in you will carry it on to completion until the day of Christ Jesus' (Phil. 1:6).

Chapter 9

Sitting Ducks or an Army on the Offensive?

So far we have observed different aspects of the occult and seen some of the reasons why people are so fascinated by it. Fascination generally leads to involvement which in turn leads to danger, spiritual bondage and darkness.

Satan has no friends, and those who involve themselves in the occult, or who are spiritually blind, certainly pose no threat to him. In one sense they are on his side, merely pawns in his strategy. From his perspective they are a disposable commodity within his effort to win a battle that is already lost. The greatest threat, in Satan's mind, is clearly posed by all those who have responded to Jesus Christ and become Christians. They have now transferred their allegiance to the kingdom of God and as a result can exercise spiritual authority over the powers of darkness.

Because of this threat, Satan is in entrenched war against all Christians. If there is any way that he can wound, maim or wreck their spiritual effectiveness he surely will. Despite this venomous mission, he is unable to influence our final destiny, nor can he snatch us away from God's hand.

> My sheep listen to my voice; I know them, and they follow
> me. I give them eternal life, and they shall never perish;
> no-one can snatch them out of my hand. My Father, who
> has given them to me, is greater than all; no-one can snatch
> them out of my Father's hand (Jn. 10:27–29).

Satan, in the words of Peter, is the '*enemy*' (1 Pet. 5:8). He
is utterly committed to the ruining of all life, especially the
life of God's children. However, as committed Christians,
we will continually frustrate Satan's efforts because he is
unable to get at us as we stand firm in our faith.

In the light of this, only the foolish Christian will
contemplate wandering from God's ways and into the
place of vulnerability where he can be picked off by the
enemy. Rebellion against God in this context is rather like
walking down the middle of a street in broad daylight
when you know a sniper is after you. Your only hope is
that he's a lousy shot!

Because Satan knows his authority is limited, only on
rare occasions will he stage an outright attack against the
alert Christian. Such attacks generally blow his cover,
meet with head-on opposition, and end ultimately with
his defeat.

As a result, the guerrilla or terrorist style is normally
employed as he seeks to bring as much suffering and
destruction as he can into the world.

This battle scenario makes it all-important for the
Christian to be sure of where they stand. A sound footing
will ensure that there are no slip-ups when the wind of
adversity begins to blow. Alongside this, we need to be
equipped to anticipate the nature of enemy attack. A study
of past skirmishes and installation of radar (of the spiritual
variety!) will hopefully remove the element of surprise
from the picture. A familiarity with God's armour is also
invaluable. These subjects will be our theme for the rest
of the chapter.

Plugging the Gaps

When I was a teenager I used to have a clinker-built rowing boat moored beside one of my local lakes. It was great for messing about in and ideal for fishing. But despite its usefulness, the boat had one or two design faults. The main one was the drainage plug. This device could be pulled out of the bottom of the boat from the inside, allowing rainwater to be drained from the boat prior to launching out into the lake. All of this sounded absolutely fine in theory, until I realised that the plug didn't fit properly and would often pop out while I was on the lake! After a few minutes, I would experience a sinking feeling, followed by furious bailing and a simultaneous search for the offending plug!

As Christians, we are destined for a victorious life in Jesus Christ. Although not immune to a little buffeting every now and then, we can override whatever adverse waves either the enemy or circumstances may throw at us. Our problem is neither the willingness nor the ability of God to help, but is often our own plugholes.

These are the deficiencies and weaknesses that exist in both our character and our relationship with God. If left undealt with, these weaknesses can become points of access for the enemy. Plug your gaps or else the sinking feeling may develop into something a little more serious.

A plug to fit the gap

When I first left school I found a job in the Civil Service. I remember at one of my periodic assessments, my boss sat me down to review my performance during the preceding six months. His concluding comments were, 'Well, Roger, you seem to be a square peg in a round hole.' I lacked the two main qualifications: a love of red tape and the ability to do the job without asking too many awkward questions!

I just did not fit the mould and so my job performance was somewhat leaky.

The only way to avoid leakage is to get the right plug. Within our lives we need to know that God is able to plug all our gaps. He is more than able to heal our weaknesses and give us complete fulfilment. The apostle Paul puts it another way, saying: 'For in Christ all the fullness of the Deity lives in bodily form, and you have been given fullness in Christ, who is the head over every power and authority' (Col. 2:9,10)

Each one of us as Christians can find wholeness in Jesus Christ, because of who he is, and also because of his death and resurrection. In fact one of the meanings of the word 'salvation' is wholeness. All God requires is that we respond to his love, giving our lives over to him on an ongoing basis. God, as Creator, is the source of all love, joy and peace. The root of meaning is found in him personally. We can trust this loving Father to supply all our needs out of his vast and tremendous resources.

Getting plugged!

Upon becoming Christians, we are firmly established as God's children with all the amazing benefits that entails. It's like suddenly discovering we are joint heirs of a vast kingdom. This kingdom has many riches and covers an area of spectacular and varied landscape.

The full benefits of this inheritance will only be enjoyed through long periods of time on safari by Land Rover and on foot. Much would also be gained from a helicopter-style overview. The landscape will need to be studied as we learn to enjoy its produce, as well as taking time out to be with the other citizens of the kingdom. All in all, it would be quite an exciting and challenging exercise.

As Christians we have in fact become heirs with a massive inheritance (see Gal. 4:7). We need to take time out to fully experience it. Part of this inheritance is having many of the empty holes in our lives plugged by God's forgiving and healing power. Becoming a Christian makes a difference to the whole of our being. We have not been left by God to lead a life of endless religious observance, devoid of all feeling and the concrete experience of his power. Far from it! Jesus Christ came to give us life, and life we will get!

This rich inheritance has many aspects, each fitting exactly into different parts of our being. Let's look and see how these help us in some of our everyday struggles. These two brief examples are areas of difficulty used often by the enemy to paralyse us in our walk with God.

1. *Guilt and condemnation.* There are two types of guilt. One is brought about by the Holy Spirit leading us Godward to find faith and receive forgiveness (Jn. 16:8, 9). The other is produced both by our own wounded consciences and also by Satan himself. His aim is to keep us in guilt, alienated from God, despite the fact that we have long been forgiven and the slate has been wiped clean.

In the first instance, guilt or conviction is a healthy state to be in as it causes us to recognise sin for what is – *sin*! We can then go to God and get the whole thing sorted out. For example, after a bad day I may return home and be particularly rude, frosty and generally obnoxious to my wife. Then I may sit down and begin to feel bad about the way I've treated her – and so I should! However, this guilt should only be a temporary experience. As I go and apologise to her, I receive her forgiveness, our relationship is completely restored and the feelings of guilt become history. This is the way things should work in our walk with God. Read 1 John 1:9 if you don't believe me.

We must learn firstly to recognise our sin, and secondly to bring it to the Lord for forgiveness and cleansing. After this we must learn to walk free of it and not be continually harping back to the past which God has dealt with ages ago.

It is often at this stage that the enemy begins to sow lies into our minds like: 'God hasn't really forgiven you' 'You're not worth forgiving' or 'You're just useless and good for nothing.'

We must learn to get a hold of these thoughts and expel them from our minds. The Bible encourages us to take each thought captive (2 Cor. 10:5) This basically means that we must learn to think God's thoughts and what he thinks about us rather than believe the lies of the enemy. This will mean developing self-control in the whole area of our thought life.

The problem for some Christians is that they believe anything about themselves provided it's not in the Bible! We must resist these impulses and come to a knowledge of God's truth which will set us free.

The truth is that as Christians we have access to freedom from guilt and condemnation (judgement).

We have no need to fear because Jesus Christ was judged on our behalf when he died upon the cross. We can now enjoy forgiveness and live in freedom from condemnation.

> Let us draw near to God with a sincere heart in full assurance of faith, having our hearts sprinkled to cleanse us from a guilty conscience and having our bodies washed with pure water (Heb. 10:22).

> Therefore, there is now no condemnation for those who are in Christ Jesus (Rom. 8:1).

2. *Fear.* Again, there are two types of fear. One is good and healthy, while the other is an absolute paralyser. I want to concentrate on the latter, but first let me make a couple of

comments about the first variety. The healthy fear is the fear of the Lord. In fact, the writer of Proverbs declares that the fear of the Lord is the beginning of all wisdom and true understanding (see Prov. 9:10). This fear is basically an awe, respect and worship of a mighty, all-powerful God. This attitude means we are not about to take his blessing for granted; neither are we about to provoke his anger as we know we can count on him to discipline us! (Read Heb. 12:5–12.)

Although we are his children and can approach him as Father with boldness, excitement and intimacy, there is an element of awe and respect which must be present. This fear of the Lord is very healthy and to be encouraged.

However, all other fears are outside of this category. While we may experience fear if we consciously sin against God, it is never his will for us to be in fear. Fears of people, death, Satan, the dark, heights, water and all other types of fear and phobia can be expelled and healed by the power of the Holy Spirit. If you have ever experienced a very strong fear due to occult involvement or past trauma, hopefully you will have already had it dealt with in response to Chapter 8! We need to know, however, that not all our fears fall into this category.

Some are just due to the fact that we are mortal human beings, while others are provoked by the world around us. Plunging stock markets, terminal diseases, unemployment and other much talked about issues mean that many people operate continually at the fear level. This need not be our experience as Christians: 'For you did not receive a spirit that makes you a slave again to fear, but you received the Spirit of sonship. And by him we cry, "*Abba*, Father"' (Rom. 8:15).

We have been adopted into God's family and as a result can know him intimately as Daddy. There is closeness which involves his absolute acceptance as well as the protection of his everlasting arms, and there's not a safer place in the universe.

We have received the Holy Spirit, and as we are filled with him so we will be filled with God's love and released from our fears. This was the experience the psalmist who sought after the Lord and was delivered from *all* his fears (Ps. 34:4–7). It has also been the experience of millions of Christians throughout the ages.

> And so we know and rely on the love God has for us. God is love. Whoever lives in love lives in God, and God in him. Love is made complete among us so that we will have confidence on the day of judgment, because in this world we are like him. There is no fear in love. But perfect love drives out fear, because fear has to do with punishment. The man who fears is not made perfect in love (1 Jn. 4:16–18).

Say no more!

These brief examples are just the tip of the iceberg as far as our inheritance in Christ is concerned. I'll leave you with the exciting task of investigating the other aspects of your inheritance personally. Suffice to say that, whether our problems differ from the above or not, we can be assured of God's ability to meet our needs.

According to God's word, when we became Christians we also became overcomers of this world. We need no longer be weighed down and crushed by the many fears and snares of this age which seem to engulf so many people. While we face difficulty, we need to maintain our faith and trust in God. We have become new creations (2 Cor. 5:17), changed people, and as such can learn to respond in victory to trial and tribulation. We need no longer be under the circumstances, but can rise over them because of the work of the Holy Spirit in us.

According to the apostle Paul, we have become more than conquerors. This basically means that we can cope with our problems with plenty of room to spare. No problem, regardless of its size, has the power to separate us from the love of God (Rom. 8:31–39).

Get Your Armour On!

Having looked at strengthening the defence lines of our personal lives, let's look further at the vast spiritual armoury we have as Christians.

> Finally, be strong in the Lord and in his mighty power. Put on the full armour of God so that you can take your stand against the devil's schemes. For our struggle is not against flesh and blood, but against the rulers, against the authorities, against the powers of this dark world and against the spiritual forces of evil in the heavenly realms. Therefore put on the full armour of God, so that when the day of evil comes, you may be able to stand your ground, and after you have done everything, to stand. Stand firm then, with the belt of truth buckled around your waist, with the breastplate of righteousness in place, and with your feet fitted with the readiness that comes from the gospel of peace. In addition to all this, take up the shield of faith, with which you can extinguish all the flaming arrows of the evil one. Take the helmet of salvation and the sword of the Spirit, which is the word of God. And pray in the Spirit on all occasions with all kinds of prayers and requests. With this in mind, be alert and always keep on praying for all the saints (Eph. 6:10–18).

Here we have a classic passage on the whole subject of spiritual warfare. Get to grips with this and I guarantee that your whole life will be changed!

As Christians, whether we like it or not, we are in a battle. Ignoring Satan will not make him go away. Far from it. If he's out of sight and out of mind he will be allowed to operate behind the scenes of our lives. You have a choice which involves two options.

One is to take the attitude of the passive, non-involved believer living the careless life of lukewarm Christianity. As such you will be a Christian of the sitting duck variety. You are in a position to be hit by much of what the enemy throws at you, as well as being largely ineffective as a soldier or follower of Jesus Christ.

The other option is to enlist in God's army. This means taking the Christian life seriously and resolving to stand alongside other believers in determined, offensive faith, praying 'your kingdom come'. This will involve seeing God's victory unveiled in your own personal struggles and the lives of others, as well as society at large.

There are no qualifications required to enlist in God's army. In fact all those who have received the free gift of eternal life have been freely drafted in! Don't go AWOL (Absent Without Leave); you may miss a vital part of God's whole purpose for your life.

In the Ephesians passage, we are encouraged to be 'strong in the Lord and in his mighty power'. This would be a great comfort because, while the thought of being strong involves an assertion of the muscle of truth, it is clear that it is in *God's* mighty power that we are strong. In one sense, the battle is the Lord's (see 2 Chr. 20:1–30, especially verse 15). Alongside this we are instructed to put on the full armour of God. This word 'full' (Greek word *panoplia*) means 'full armour of a heavy-laden soldier'. This armour originates from God himself. It is given to us by him, it is designed by him and as such is totally effective in battle. It has none of the design faults that would characterise armour of human origin.

Alongside this we are reminded of our enemy, or enemies. They are supernatural, powerful beings who have authority (see the Kingdom of Evil table in Chapter 3). We have been given spiritual armour to equip us for the spiritual battle in the heavenly realms. Only as we recognise this and stand firm in God do we have any hope of thwarting the devil's schemes (plans or strategies). Standing firm involves coming to a confident knowledge and experience of our faith whereby we won't be wobbling when the time of pressure, difficulty or testing arrives ('the day of evil', Eph. 6:13).

We have been equipped for a struggle (Eph. 6:12). We stand in the place of victory and triumph (in Christ), but will still have to struggle, persist and be determined, both in prayer and our practical service to God, if we are to see God's victory revealed with increasing visibility on the earth. Christians who are expecting a spiritual picnic have not quite grasped the depth of God's call upon their lives. A struggle involves exertion, effort and discipline.

As we will now see, the armour God has given is not just Sunday wear, neither is it merely to be worn during the day and discarded for 'jimmy jams' at night! The complete soldier of Jesus Christ keeps himself covered at all times and is not going to be caught short with nothing but his teddy bear to throw at the enemy! Let's now get to grips with the armour at our disposal.

Paul spent many hours in prison due to his preaching of the gospel. As a result, he would have had plenty of time to observe the finer details of the armour worn by his Roman guards. As he did this, he drew spiritual parallels which have proved invaluable to Christians throughout the ages.

The belt

We are first introduced to the belt of truth which is to be buckled firmly around our waist. This belt held the whole of the Roman soldier's armour in place. The scabbard for the sword was placed on it and it was also crucial in holding the breastplate in position. As well as this, it held the soldier's tunic up. If not done up tightly, the soldier could suddenly end up with the lot round his ankles, right in the middle of a battle!

According to Paul, our spiritual belt is truth. This truth has two aspects to it:

1. A clear appreciation and knowledge of who God is and who we are in the light of salvation. We see the world from the perspective revealed in the Scriptures.

2. We are truthful, sincere and have integrity in our own personal life. It is all very well having the right doctrine, but what good is that if we are living lives full of hypocrisy and double standards? We must be truthful and clear in our standing before God, inviting him to search us and know our hearts (Ps. 139:23, 24). Only then will the belt of truth be firmly in place and will we be secure against enemy attack.

The breastplate

The breastplate was a strong, solid piece of armour which protected all of the vital organs in the upper part of the body. It could be said that it protected the heart of a person. For the Christian, this breastplate is righteousness. Like truth, this righteousness has two aspects:

1. The sense of being right, pure and justified before God. This is not as a result of our own efforts, but is a righteousness given to us by God himself: 'God made him who had no sin to be sin for us, so that in him we might become the righteousness of God'

(2 Cor. 5:21). Jesus took our sin upon the cross and it was replaced in our lives by something we could never earn: the righteousness of God. This breastplate will encourage us to advance boldly in God, and not take any of Satan's slanderous accusations to heart. Especially the ones that say we are not good enough.

2. The second aspect of this is moral purity in our own lives. We need to be in the habit of keeping short accounts with our heavenly Father. We must be in the position where any known sin has already been confessed, cleansed and forgiven. Otherwise, if our life is being lived in moral confusion and disobedience to God, our breastplate will be out of place. We will be vulnerable to the enemy.

The footwear

It seems certain that Paul had in mind the *caliga* or half boots normally worn by the Roman legionary. These were made of leather, the toes left free, with heavy studded soles and fastened to the ankles and shins by straps. They were solid and equipped the soldier for long and enduring marches. The studs ensured a firm footing would be maintained even in a furious combat situation.

These shoes stand for the solid firmness and enduring qualities given by God to all those who believe wholeheartedly in him. Such people are not prone to the instability and slip-ups experienced by others. Along with these shoes comes a readiness to announce the good news of God's kingdom (see Is. 52:7; Col. 4:2–6). The devil hates evangelism, and the Christian who is on the offensive in this area creates all kinds of problems for him.

The shield

This was a strong, well-made and vital part of the armour. It was large and oblong in shape and covered the whole person. It was used to deflect blows from the enemy swords, as well as to deflect and extinguish flaming arrows that were often fired by enemy archers.

Satan will continually be firing arrows of rebellion, fear, accusations, as well as temptations towards sin. Faith is our shield to counter these attacks. With faith we are able to lay hold of God's promises and take shelter in him: 'Consequently, faith comes from hearing the message, and the message is heard through the word of Christ' (Rom. 10:17).

Obviously if our shield of faith is to be effective, firstly, we need to know the promises, and secondly, we need to *trust* them actively. As one commentator observed, 'Faith is a lively and reckless confidence in the grace of God!' Our trust in God must be wholehearted and in the right sense reckless.

The helmet

The Roman helmet was usually made of a tough metal, like bronze or iron. It was padded on the inside with felt or sponge to make the weight bearable. Sometimes it was fastened by straps that extended down over the ears and under the chin. In some cases a hinged visor added frontal protection. These heavier helmets were so solid that nothing short of an axe or hammer could pierce them.

The helmet is called salvation and covers the mind, reasoning and particularly the thought life. Salvation includes assurance that we have been saved, that we are in an ongoing relationship with God now and are assured of a secure eternal future with the Lord Jesus Christ. When our minds are covered by these wonderful facts we are supremely protected.

The sword

This sword (*Machaira*) was not the long sword, but was the short sword of the close personal encounter. This was both an offensive and defensive weapon of devastating effectiveness. Paul calls this sword of the Spirit the 'word of God'. He is clearly referring to the truth of God (as revealed in Scripture) when spoken under the power of the Holy Spirit. Jesus himself used Scripture when in confrontation with the devil in Matthew chapter 4. It is worth noting at this stage that the devil also used Scripture, to attack Jesus. However, his usage was twisted, incorrect and out of context. We need to take a leaf out of Jesus' book and learn to use God's word as a defensive weapon against the enemy.

God's word is also effective when used on the offensive: 'For the word of God is living and active. Sharper than any double-edged sword, it penetrates even to dividing soul and spirit, joints and marrow; it judges the thoughts and attitudes of the heart' (Heb. 4:12). Not only does it trouble the enemy, but it is also extremely effective when used in evangelism as it cuts deep into the hearts of its hearers.

The person armed with the sword of the Spirit has a light, mobile and effective weapon. It is effective defensively and is devastating when used on the offensive.

In conclusion to this passage, Paul recommends prayer in the Spirit. All our spiritual armour must be married with prayer to obtain maximum effectiveness. Prayer is diverse, exciting and varied. 'All kinds of prayers and requests' can be carried out 'on all occasions'. In prayer we have the authority to bind the work of Satan. This means that through our prayers he is restricted, and those under his power can be loosed or released (see Mt. 12:29; 18:18).

Similarly, as we submit to God we are called to resist and stand against all the works of evil through prayer and spiritual warfare (Jas. 4:7; 1 Pet. 5:9). As Christians we should all learn to engage carefully in this area. It is only as the powers of darkness are driven back that the work of God will be able to grow to its full potential.

Chapter 10

Where is the Real Action?

So far in this book we have examined the occult and seen how Satan's power has clearly been broken by the power of Christ. From the outside, the apparent excitement of occult phenomena may seem alluring.

However, we have seen the truth of the matter. The occult is dangerous, damaging, and Satan is the insidious enemy of all that is truly good, pleasurable and worth living for.

It is good to see the effectiveness of God's armour and also to touch briefly on the tremendous power that is produced when Christians engage in effective prayer. Unfortunately, outsiders observing the Christian church at large would often not see or be confronted by this power. They have been deceived into thinking that Christianity is just a rotting corpse, a dose of pious attitudes and compromised morality.

In the face of this, it is not hard to understand why Christianity is often viewed as boring or dead spiritually. Nothing, of course, could be further from the truth. Since I first became a Christian I have realised the tremendous joy, purpose and excitement that was mine through my relationship with Jesus Christ. On top of the wholeness and forgiveness he brought to me I also received his Holy

Spirit which has enabled me to grow into a life full of meaning and spiritual experience that hitherto I had no idea even existed.

My relationship with God is supernatural, in the sense that at times it operates outside of things which can be explained by natural laws. Some Christians would be wary of calling their faith supernatural for fear of occult connotations. As long as we stand firm in Christ and are under the authority of Scripture there is no danger of that. Our relationship with God is to be in spirit and in truth (Jn. 4:24). The spiritual aspect can be out of balance and dangerous unless regulated by Scripture. Similarly, the Scriptures themselves are dead unless they are enlivened and illumined by the Holy Spirit. Having said this, if we believe in prayer, what could be more supernatural than a prayer answered? On top of answered prayer, I have known the experience of the presence of God with me daily, his healing and delivering power, I have also seen the gifts of the Holy Spirit operating genuinely and effectively on many occasions. My experience is nothing unique; it is shared by millions upon millions of believers throughout the world today. God is supernatural. The Christian has the tremendous privilege of relationship with him at that level.

Introducing the Holy Spirit

We experience God's presence through the person and work of the Holy Spirit. He was sent to empower us after Jesus ascended to be with God the Father following his resurrection. Notice the Bible always refers to the Holy Spirit as a person and never as an impersonal force. This is part of the great scriptural mystery of the Trinity, whereby God is one yet three persons: Father, Son and Holy Spirit.

In John chapter 14, Jesus teaches along these lines, clearly saying that anyone who had seen him had seen God the Father. Jesus Christ is God. He then adds to the fact of his oneness with the Father, saying that he is also one with the Holy Spirit, the Counsellor who will be with us and in us (v. 17). Because Father, Son and Holy Spirit are one, it is true to say that Jesus is in the Father, we are in Christ (through salvation) and that Christ is in us by the Holy Spirit (v. 20).

There are other passages that also firmly establish that the Holy Spirit is God. It is interesting to note, for instance, that the work of creation is attributed to all three persons of the Trinity. Namely, God (Gen. 1:1), Jesus Christ (Col. 1:16) and the Holy Spirit (Gen. 1:2).

My aim here is not to prove the Trinity, but to point out that Christian spiritual experience is a totally different ball game to the occult. It is not the manipulation of dark forces, neither is it a kind of oneness with some kind of energy or force present in creation. True spiritual life begins at salvation, which involves repentance, faith and receiving the gift of the Holy Spirit (Acts 2:38). We do not in any sense possess power, rather we ourselves, through salvation, belong to God, the source of all spiritual strength. Therefore, when we as Christians experience the power of the Holy Spirit, we do so because of God's generous gift and not because of our own power. In fact we have no power of our own: our dependence is entirely upon God. However, this should not make us feel in any way insecure for we know that God is totally faithful and utterly trustworthy (Ps. 146:6).

Let's now spend the rest of this chapter seeing a little of some of the exciting things the Holy Spirit brings to the life of the Christian. He brings:

1. *Counsel* (Jn. 14:16–18)

The Holy Spirit is the Counsellor. As we open ourselves to God he will be our Teacher and help us to grow in faith. He will open the Bible to us which will help us to know God more and keep our lives on a straight path.

2. *Assurance*

He is the seal of God's ownership of our lives (Eph. 1:13, 14). As we experience his life in us we know we belong to God; we have his seal of approval. As we pray he cries out 'Daddy' within us and we know that we have become God's children, his heirs with an inheritance (Rom. 8:15–17). We can now have a deep experience of God's fatherhood because of the Holy Spirit's work.

3. *Conviction* (Jn. 16:8–11)

It is the Holy Spirit's job to work in the world, showing people where they are in sin in order that they can put it right with God and find his forgiveness. If we are open, he will show us when we've slipped up and also reveal to us the way we should be living. Alongside this, he assures us of Satan's condemnation, judgement and defeat. As a result of this, our faith in God and his victory becomes stronger.

4. *Fruit* (Gal. 5:22–23)

When we become Christians there is often a huge gulf between our lifestyle and character, and God's will for us. Our job is to submit ourselves to Jesus as Lord and exert our wills to co-operate with the Holy Spirit who now lives in us. He will then begin to miraculously reshape our character and bring God's life and holiness to us. He will not want to turn us into religious clones; rather he will make us the best *individuals* possible!

5. *Glory to Father and Son* (Jn. 16:14)

He will continually be pointing not to himself but to the Lord Jesus and to our heavenly Father. All of his work in us, whether in assurance, character or the gifts of the Holy Spirit, must have this characteristic of giving credit, worship and glory to the Father and Son. If this element is not present we need to ask whether it is really the Holy Spirit who is at work. His job is predominantly to focus worship on the Father and Son. However, the angels sing 'Holy, holy, holy is the Lord' (Rev. 4:8). It is therefore perfectly okay to, on occasions, sing, worship and also pray to the Holy Spirit, because he is God.

6. *Spiritual Life* (Jn. 7:38–39)

Where there has been dryness, hunger, thirst and searching, the Holy Spirit will come and fill the Christian to overflowing with joy and fulfilment What's more, it is an endless supply that will be continually welling up inside us. It is a taste of the eternal life which we will experience either after physical death or when Jesus Christ returns, whichever happens first (see 1 Thess. 4:13–18).

7. *Power* (Acts 1:8)

The Christian is not left powerless in the face of today's society. God has given us the Holy Spirit and *we* have received the power and ability to be his witnesses. When filled with the Holy Spirit, the otherwise fearful disciples found strength and boldness to tell others about Jesus – even in the face of extreme persecution. One of the main proofs that we are filled with God's Spirit is certainly the presence of boldness when speaking of Jesus Christ to others. However, his power went further than inspired bravery and the spoken word. The church was enabled to truly carry on the ministry of Jesus through miracles of healing (Acts 3:1–10), signs and wonders (Acts 5:12, 8:26–40), casting out demons (Acts 8:4–8) as well as the other gifts of the Holy Spirit like tongues (Acts 2:4) and prophecy (Acts 21:10,11). As a result of this outpouring of the Holy Spirit, many thousands of people became Christians and joined the church. It is the same Holy Spirit present in Christians today who indwelt the

New Testament Christians. As we trust in God and step forward in faith, we too can be used supernaturally, just as those in the early church were.

Be Filled and Equipped

All those who have believed in Jesus Christ have received the Holy Spirit. However, God's will for us is that we are filled to overflowing in him so that we can experience the reality of his power dynamically in our lives. Once filled with the Spirit, we have access to a whole new dimension of the Christian life, particularly in the realm of the supernatural. But we must remember that we are encouraged to go on being filled with the Holy Spirit on a continuous basis (Eph. 5:18). This was certainly the experience of those in the early church who were filled again and again after their initial baptism in the Spirit at Pentecost (Acts 4:8, 31).

It is God's desire to fill every Christian to overflowing with his power. The gift is free; all you need to do is desire to be filled, trust in God, ask to be filled and you will surely receive (Lk. 11:13). If you have any difficulty in this area, why not go and talk to a mature Christian who is already baptised in the spirit and ask him to pray for you in this respect.

Once filled with the Holy Spirit, we become more aware of his work in our life at every level. Praying in the Spirit becomes much easier, and our faith, when continually exercised, will be steadily growing. Also, we will find ourselves experiencing the gifts of the Holy Spirit. Now, these are gifts or manifestations of the same Holy Spirit, each gift having a different function and purpose, just as the fruit of the Holy Spirit is one fruit with nine flavours. So the gifts are different workings of the same Spirit.

Each gift is designed to meet a specific need at a specific time.

In the light of the counterfeit supernatural gifts displayed by the occultist, it is particularly important for the Christian to understand the gifts of the Holy Spirit and to be able to use them for God's glory. These gifts will build up the church, strengthen you personally, as well as inspiring other people to faith in Christ. While there are no doubt many questions concerning the gifts that I could address, I want to spend the rest of this chapter giving a brief summary of the gifts outlined in 1 Corinthians chapter 12. I hope this will help you to gain a deeper understanding and experience of them in your own life.

Now about spiritual gifts, brothers, I do not want you to be ignorant. You know that when you were pagans, somehow or other you were influenced and led astray to dumb idols. Therefore I tell you that no-one who is speaking by the Spirit of God says, 'Jesus be cursed,' and no-one can say, 'Jesus is Lord,' except by the Holy Spirit.

There are different kinds of gifts, but the same Spirit. There are different kinds of service, but the same Lord. There are different kinds of working, but the same God works all of them in all men.

Now to each one the manifestation of the Spirit is given for the common good. To one there is given through the Spirit the message of wisdom, to another the message of knowledge by means of the same Spirit, to another faith by the same Spirit, to another gifts of healing by that one Spirit, to another miraculous powers, to another prophecy, to another the ability to distinguish between spirits, to another the ability to speak in different kinds of tongues, and to still another the interpretation of tongues. All these are the work of one and the same Spirit, and he gives them to each one, just as he determines (1 Cor. 12:1–11).

The gifts are:

Wisdom (v. 8)

This is not logic or common sense, but is wisdom with a supernatural origin. Jesus showed this remarkable kind of wisdom when dealing with the woman caught in adultery (see Jn. 8:1–11). He was faced with a genuine dilemma. The woman was caught in adultery, and under the law of Moses she should have been stoned. It was clearly not his desire to consent to her stoning, yet if he didn't he could have been accused of being a lawbreaker. His response was: 'If any one of you is without sin, let him be the first to throw a stone at her' (v. 7). This was ingenious in that it dispelled the crowd, leaving him to pronounce forgiveness and lead the woman away from her sinful life.

Another example of such wisdom can be found through Solomon in 1 Kings 3:16–28. There are many examples in the Scriptures of God unveiling truth, not by natural means, but through the work of the Holy Spirit (see Mt. 16:14–17). The word of wisdom is this type of unveiling.

Word of knowledge (v. 8)

This gift involves the revealing of something about a situation or a person that could not have been known through rational observation. Jesus displays this perfectly in John 4:17–19: '"I have no husband," she replied. Jesus said to her, "You are right when you say you have no husband. The fact is, you have had five husbands, and the man you now have is not your husband. What you have just said is quite true."'

We need to note firstly the sensitivity with which Jesus used this gift, and how despite its personal nature it served to spread the gospel and draw more people to Jesus: 'Then, leaving her water jar, the woman went back to the town and said to the people, "Come, see a man who

told me everything I ever did. Could this be the Christ?"
They came out of the town and made their way towards
him' (Jn. 4:28–30).

A good example of this gift operating today was when
one of the girls on the leadership team of our church had
lunch with a friend, who was not a Christian. During the
meal she felt strongly that her friend was burdened by a
feeling of being an orphan. She gently suggested this to
her, saying that God wanted to be her heavenly Father
and receive her into his family. The girl was flabbergasted
because not only were these thoughts on her mind, but
unbeknown to my friend, the girl was literally an orphan!
The word of knowledge opened the door for God's
love to flow in and after a short time the girl became a
Christian.

Faith (v. 9)

This is not the faith involved in becoming a Christian,
although this faith is in one sense also a gift from God
(Eph. 2:8, 9; Acts 16:31). The faith mentioned here is a gift to
believe for something out of the ordinary. It may be given
in order that we may come to terms with a crisis situation
or to reach for something miraculous.

Two examples of this are, firstly, the insistence of Elisha
in believing that God was going to whisk Elijah away from
the earth supernaturally in spite of the circumstances (2
Kgs. 2). Secondly, we have the example of the centurion in
Matthew 8:5–13. So strong was his faith that Jesus only had
to declare his servant healed and he was utterly convinced,
even though Jesus had never actually met the servant!

If you want to learn more about the exploits of faith,
read Hebrews chapter 11 and then look up all the names
of the heroes of faith in a Bible concordance. Find the
passages that cover their lives and read them thoughtfully.
You will find it very inspiring!

Healing (v. 9)

This is not healing through medicine – not that there is anything wrong with healing brought about this way! Here we are talking about healing through the power of the Holy Spirit. There are numerous scriptural examples of this, including Jesus with the leper (Mt. 8:1–4) and the paralytic (Mt. 9:1–8), as well as Peter with the crippled beggar (Acts 3:1–10).

This also includes not just physical healing, but healing of the mind and emotions. Again, this type of healing should not be confused with psychology, or endless counselling, but is supernatural, involving the work of God's power bringing wholeness directly into a person's life.

I must admit that within our church I would like to see more of this gift revealed. However, over the years we have seen the healing of a broken limb, torn ligaments (crutches carried home!), cancer, stomach ulcers, eye problems, asthma, eczema, partial deafness as well as fears, phobias and emotional problems. God has gifts of healing he wants to pass on to many sick people. Are we prepared to move out and pray in faith to see these gifts passed on?

Miracles (v. 10)

This is the performing of supernatural signs that are out of the ordinary. Biblical examples of this include Elisha with the oil in the jars (2 Kgs. 4:1–7), Jesus turning the water into wine (Jn. 2:1–11) and Jesus and Peter walking on the water (Mt. 14:28–32). Also in Acts 8:39, 40 we see Philip being miraculously transported from one place to another!

This is a spiritual gift which seems to be quite rare, especially in the European church. I am sure that this is not due to any reluctance on God's part to move miraculously. I believe it is mainly due to our rationalistic and materialistic world-view which strangles faith and promotes unbelief.

Most of us are rarely in a position of sufficient faith and openness to be given the gift of miracles.

I can't say that I have ever been used miraculously to the extent that our biblical examples display. However, I have regularly experienced God's miraculous provision in the area of finance. I remember one particular instance when my church needed a large sum of money to enable us to complete a particular project. After prayer we received the *exact* amount we needed from a source totally outside our sphere of contact! It arrived just in the nick of time, and we were all extremely thankful to God for his kindness. While this was hardly a miracle of New Testament calibre, we've got to start somewhere!

Prophecy (v. 10)

This is a message spoken from God either to a person or a group of people. In the New Testament, for the most part, the tone of prophecy is to strengthen, encourage and comfort Christians (1 Cor. 14:3). Only on occasions will the message have anything to do with future events, for example when the prophet Agabus foretold a famine (Acts 11:28) and also the arrest of Paul in Jerusalem (Acts 21:10, 11).

It is a mistake to think that every word of prophecy is robotically received from God and thus has to be 100 per cent correct. During prophecy the Holy Spirit is working through us as fallible human beings (2 Cor. 4:7, earthen vessels) and so we prophesy 'in part' or imperfectly (1 Cor. 13:9). So, when we receive a prophecy it is important for us to draw out the heart or kernel of the message and not be put off by, say, the bad breath of the messenger!

Prophecy is a powerful and relevant gift. As a result, the apostle Paul exhorts us to 'eagerly desire spiritual gifts, especially the gift of prophecy' (1 Cor. 14:1). One of the reasons for this is perhaps because a prophetic word often speaks more directly into a situation. For instance, while we may know the doctrine of God's love and acceptance outlined in the Scriptures, at times of failure we can feel particularly useless. It is just then that the unsuspecting prophet often brings a message to us of assurance with regard to God's love and acceptance. Just what the doctor ordered!

Also, some prophecy will need to be held to one side to allow the Lord to bring it to pass if it really is from him. I remember as a relatively new Christian having a friend of mine, who was a recent convert, prophesy over me 'upon this rock I will build my church'! I wasn't sure how to handle it. I assumed that my friend had got over-excited and what the Lord really meant was that I should involve myself in the leadership of the youth group!

However, four years later I ended up starting a church with around twenty friends. Now, years later, we have been involved in planting a number of other churches and embarked on many other projects in our community and also nationally. God's plans were somewhat bigger than mine, but somehow I was better prepared for what happened because of my friend's prophecy.

Prophecy, as I've said, is mainly for strengthening and encouragement and occasionally correction or rebuke. As such we should be reluctant to make important decisions exclusively around a prophetic word. Generally, prophecy should confirm and give shape to what we already feel. It should also work alongside the spiritual counsel of mature Christian friends as well as complementing what we have already understood from the Bible. Any prophecy which contradicts scriptural truth does not have its origin in God's heart.

Prophecy can be given in different forms. For example, it can be spoken, sung, dramatised (Agabus in Acts

21:10, 11) or given in the form of visions (pictures) which
then need to be explained to their receiver.

Discerning of spirits (v. 10, see also 1 Jn. 4:1–3)

This gift has two aspects. Firstly, it is the ability to notice
when another person is under the influence of evil spirits.
Alongside this, God generally reveals which area of that
person's life needs to be dealt with in order that he can
be set free. Jesus often used this gift (see Mt. 9:32, 33) as
on occasions did Paul (Acts 16:16–18). It is particularly
important because Christians often carry on blissfully
unaware of the enemy activity going on right under their
noses!

The other side of the coin, however, is when the
enemy gets the blame for any and every problem which,
in reality, are just 'facts of life' and not of demonic
origin. The discerning Christian will be able to tell the
difference.

Discernment also covers knowing what attitude or
motive lies behind people's activity. For instance, in his
conversation with the rich young ruler (Lk. 18:18–25),
Jesus clearly saw that the obstacle blocking his salvation
was money. He was then able to apply his teaching
accordingly.

Discernment is not given to enable us to poke our noses
into people's lives and gossip about them. It is given to
help us bring love, care and freedom to them. It is for their
benefit and not ours.

Tongues (v. 10)

When in praise our human words run out, the gift of
tongues takes us further into God's presence. They can
be sung or spoken (1 Cor. 14:15) and are a beautiful way of
allowing the Holy Spirit to move us into a deeper sense of
worship. Similarly, in prayer, tongues can help in spiritual

warfare as well as general prayer as we allow the Holy Spirit to move through us in this way.

Tongues are a heavenly language and as such cannot normally be understood in the way that a normal language can, unless they are interpreted. Having said this, a friend told me that at a meeting he attended a person whose only language was English, prayed in tongues and a non-Christian behind him was astounded to hear a message in fluent Latin! As you can imagine, this surprised both the speaker and the hearer!

Speaking in tongues provides tremendous strength and builds up the life of any Christian. While it is not so important in the life of the church as a gift like prophecy, it is still nevertheless important.

Interpretation of tongues (v. 10)

Not every tongue needs to be interpreted either in our personal prayer and worship times or during the meeting of the whole church. For instance, if everyone in the congregation is singing or praying in tongues simultaneously it would take a week to hear all the interpretations! However, if a tongue is given out solo, and addressed to the whole congregation, it requires an interpretation.

Interpretation is not translation, but is an explanation of the basic sense or feel of the tongues. Therefore, it is by no means unusual for the interpretation to seem longer or shorter than the original tongue. The heart of the message is the same. Sometimes the explanation may take the form of a prayer of thanksgiving to God, while on other occasions it may be a message to the church in a similar vein to a prophecy.

It is exciting to know that there are so many ways in which God wants to move in us by his Holy Spirit. Far from being in a spiritual vacuum we will find the Christian life dynamic and full of excitement as we give ourselves to God in humility and openness.

I have no space here to give advice on how to begin moving in these gifts. I hope, however, my brief descriptions of them will have whetted your appetite to find out more. Every healthy Christian will be mindful of Paul's directive to 'eagerly desire' the spiritual gifts.

Chapter 11

Beware Low-Flying Space Cadets

A wise friend of mine once observed, 'If the devil can't hold you back, he will push you over the top.' This is particularly the case in the whole area of understanding the occult and the supernatural.

While on the one hand there are clearly those who through cynicism and unbelief are being outflanked by the devil, there are clearly others who attribute far too much to him. As a result there is sometimes a fair amount of lunatic behaviour going on within the church.

If the car radiator blows it is usually attributed to an enemy attack and never to the idiot who forgot to put the water in! If the car then runs out of petrol it must be 'the Lord speaking'. Well, if he is speaking, and I doubt it, it is probably along the lines of: 'That will teach you to be more practical and put some petrol in next time!'

Such people, in my reckoning, qualify for the dubious rank of space cadet. Some of these are mere corporals prone to the occasional super-spiritual aberration, while others live their whole lives in total unreality, thus qualifying for the infamous flight lieutenant grade!

Assorted Space Cadet Tendencies

1. Preoccupation with the nebulous

Space cadets tend to go for any strange new Christian doctrine or theory, reacting against most things that smack of common sense or rationality. Paul called these controversies 'endless genealogies'. He encourages those in the church not to devote themselves to 'myths and endless genealogies. These promote controversies rather than God's work' (1 Tim. 1:4).

Spacers tend to be like the person Paul refers to in Colossians 2:18: 'Such a person goes into great detail about what he has seen, and his unspiritual mind puffs him up with idle notions.' We must be careful at all times to ensure that what is 'felt in the spirit' (to quote the Christian cliché) actually firmly checks out against a sound and mature interpretation of the Scriptures.

These strange theories seem to emerge particularly in relation to the Second Coming or return of Jesus Christ. People spend so much time in speculation that they miss totally the Great Commission given by Christ to all believers – that is, to preach the gospel to all nations, making disciples of Jesus Christ (Mt. 28:19). Hand in hand with this often goes a rather strange way of understanding the Bible. I remember one extremely excited girl telling me that the rider on the white horse (Rev. 19) was God's promise to her of a husband, a kind of knight in shining armour! Unfortunately, she was not so amused when I gently told her that the rider was actually a picture of Jesus Christ returning to judge the earth!

Spacers like obscure prophecies and tend to spend lots of time focusing on 'new revelations' rather than focusing on the basics of knowing Jesus and living out the simple life of a follower of Jesus as we see it portrayed in the New Testament.

2. *Difficulty relating in everyday language*

With some people you need a King James dictionary with glossary to understand all the religious clichés. I always get confused because I can never work out whether, 'Bless you, bro,' means, 'Excuse me please, I want to get by', 'I can't think of anything to say', or, 'This is a boring conversation'.

I remember one unfortunate evening attending a businessmen's evangelistic dinner. During the worship the words to the songs were being put up on an overhead projector. However, there was one slight hitch: the woman with the transparencies was having a few problems and kept putting the wrong song up. The leader of the worship, obviously fuming, nervously exclaimed, 'Praise the Lord! Praise the Lord!' with each mistake.

The rough translation of this phrase, judging by the look in his eyes, was not, 'Praise to God', but, 'Silly cow!' Such super-spiritual unreality was not helping the meeting, particularly on our table where we were doing our best to hold back waves of laughter.

3. *Relational problems*

When these emerge they are normally put down to demonic activity in the life of the other person and never a character clash or the inability to relate reasonably or openly. Often the usual pleasantries like discussing the weather, sport or finding out about one another are discarded for intense discussion about the latest spiritual hot potato.

I will never forget the first charismatic meeting I attended when I experienced the classic example of how not to relate to a newcomer. I arrived somewhat nervous of what might happen, feeling right out of place. I was dressed in the standard biker gear with long hair and scruffy jeans. As I shuffled inconspicuously in at the back of the meeting I was spotted by a somewhat enthusiastic bloke on the other side of the hall. He shot across exclaiming, 'Bless you, brother,' hugged me and planted a dirty great kiss on my cheek. I was somewhat taken aback and immediately commented to my then girlfriend, 'Nice bloke, different planet!'

These are somewhat surface, sketchy and amusing caricatures of space cadet behaviour. However, I am sure that any of you who have been around in Christian circles for any length of time will recognise at least some of the things I've described.

My desire in this book is to encourage all of you to take your Christian life, spiritual warfare and the challenge of the occult seriously – to equip you to approach the issues from an informed Christian perspective with a full awareness of your standing in Christ.

However, I am anxious that everybody keeps their feet on the ground, retaining their objectivity, sense of humour and along with that their sanity! One of the ingredients often sadly lacking within teaching on these areas is common sense. If you have common sense or wisdom please hang on to it: it is a valuable commodity. If you lack it, please consider asking the Lord for some at the same time as you receive spiritual gifts (Jas. 1:5). It could save many hiccups.

My plea is that we don't kiss our brains goodbye but rather we keep our spiritual faculties intact, ensuring that they are under the lordship of Christ, tempered by a strong faith in his power. As we do this, those outside of Christianity will see the powerful truth of the gospel of Jesus Christ. They will see his power, victory and authority over the demonic realm revealed, through ordinary, reasonable and down-to-earth people with whom they can identify.

'The God of peace will soon crush Satan under your feet' (Rom. 16:20).

May this be true of all those who read this book.